When Angels Intervene

To Save The Children

of laughs. To cafe for breakfast. It's been quite a while....
Entered at airport and got letters of 'zero equals infinity'
ready to go off to newspapers, president of U.S. and etc."
(The reference is to a long, complex and hard-to-follow
statement of David's personal beliefs, titled "Zero Equals
Infinity," and to his efforts to get it read and appreciated as
he thought it deserved. The full text is reprinted in
Appendix I.)

On the 14th, Doris, Princess and the two men went sight-
seeing around Bear Lake, while David drove to Jackson Hole
to pick up Robert Harrison, a third "investor." That night
David and Princess shared Room 7 at the Sunset Motel in
Montpelier. Where the others stayed is not as clear. Doris
must have been there at some point, because she was seen by
the motel owner painting the windows of the van. David
congratulated her on the artistic effort. "This is my flower
van," she said when asked. "I'm going to paint flowers on the
windows." It was a good way to prevent people from seeing
into the van and noticing the guns and ammunition David
had inside.

The "full of fun and lots of laughs" reported by David in
his May 14th diary entry did not last long. On the morning of
Thursday the 15th, Robert Harrison said he couldn't go
through with something he "had no control over." There is
evidence that David was assembling a bomb during the time
the group stayed in Montpelier and Cokeville. The device was
triggered to blow when two pieces of metal, rigged to a
clothespin, were allowed to make contact, completing an

electrical circuit.

Perhaps Robert Harrison saw enough to know, in the short time he was a part of the group, that he was also in over his head. He told David he wanted to leave. As Bernie described it, David told her to drive Harrison to the Jackson Hole airport to "get him out of the way." This defection, whatever its cause, didn't seem to upset David very much. He may have felt Harrison didn't know enough to tell the police anything damaging.

After Robert's departure, however, David said "Thursday is not the right day." Everyone argued with him to reveal the details of the "Biggie," but he refused. Ultimately, they decided to go to Montpelier for David to rest. They checked into Rooms 130 and 131 at the Best Western Motel and relaxed the remainder of the day, just shopping and enjoying the hot tub.

Princess may have been under David's control, but, unlike Doris, she was not complacent about being there or helping him. A clerk at the Lazy T heard her make a telephone call, apparently to her fiancé in Arizona, in which she said she would come home as soon as David completed his "Biggie." "Tomorrow is the big day. ... I miss you. I'll be home soon," the clerk quoted her as saying.

Bernie understood Princess's ambivalence toward David. "Sometimes he would change his stories," Bernie said of him. "For instance, he told members of the 'group' they could back out if they wanted to. He actually let [Robert Harrison] go. I drove him to the airport myself so he could fly back to

Atlanta. But David wouldn't let the others leave the next day."

On the morning of the 16th, the group left Montpelier after eating breakfast and quaffing a few beers. Lincoln County Sheriff's Deputy Ron Hartley says that David drove along U.S. 30 and stopped to make a tape recording of exactly what his "Biggie" would entail, choosing that way to reveal his intentions to the rest of the party. Deppe and Mendenhall immediately said they could not be a part of David's "revolution." Princess, too, did not want to go along.

Whether there was much debate is unknown. Whatever happened, David didn't hesitate very long. He pulled a gun on the two men and instructed Doris and Princess to handcuff them to the inside of the van. They might refuse to cooperate, but he would make sure they couldn't interfere. David was doubly glad that Doris had painted the windows of the van. Not only the guns would be hidden from sight, but Deppe and Mendenhall as well.

Now almost everything was ready, despite the disloyalty of his "group." Lawmen conjecture that probably this same morning, possibly earlier, David visited the Cokeville dump looking for the last component he needed to finish the bomb. This was a one-gallon, plastic milk or juice jug, which he would fill with gasoline. He was proud of his sophisticated bomb, and rightly so. It was ingenious—a true product of his combined intellect and mechanical skill.

It was fitted into a two-wheel shopping cart, meticulously wired together according to written specifications. The design was intended to detonate five blasting caps, three on one shelf, two on a lower shelf, by way of an electric charge from a battery. The caps, each set into a can filled with gunpowder, aluminum dust, and flour, were designed to blow their component particles into the air like confetti. The gallon of gasoline would then explode on a delayed fuse and ignite the air-borne particles.

According to bomb experts like Sweetwater County, Wyoming's Richard Haskell, the theory of air-oxidized particles is explained in many military manuals. "The device works on the principle of a dust explosion, the type which has leveled many large grain elevators," he explained. Sprinkling a smattering of flour granules over an open flame demonstrates how highly combustible these explosions can be. Taken together, in a simultaneous and large conflagration, the results could "blow up an entire room of medium size, cave in the walls, and kill everyone in it," Haskell later emphasized. This kind of weapon is called a "deadman's bomb" because it is lethal to anyone near the bomb when it detonates. That was exactly what David wanted. With the bomb assembled and the van only a few miles from Cokeville Elementary School, David had crossed the line from eccentric philosopher and become a guerrilla warrior. He was now a very dangerous man, and he was coming with a very dangerous gift.

Princess did not share the emotions of her father. She felt like she was buckling under the strain of the last two days. At one point, David told her to move part of the van's large arsenal, perhaps away from the still-helpless Deppe and

Mendenhall. She did, but she dropped something. It did not escape the watchful eye of her father. David looked at his daughter coolly. "Screw up one more time," he announced tersely, "and I'll shoot you." She was certain he would.

Doris did not seem to question David's plans or have second thoughts about helping him. At least, she did not leave, as had Robert Harrison, or refuse to help, as had Deppe and Mendenhall. There is, however, one bit of evidence that she was not totally comfortable with plans to take over the school: "I wonder what we'll be called in the Brave New World?" reads one anxious entry in her journal.

David headed for the schoolyard, actually driving right onto the grounds. However, as all of them could see, the children were having recess. They were playing games all over, scattered actively almost all the way to the far fence. Clearly, it was not yet time to strike. Investigators believe David, with his van full of weaponry and his half-willing, half-unwilling associates, left the schoolyard and drove toward the Bear River on the west side of town, just to kill some time. Bernie Petersen says she later learned that David came to her home when she was away. Neither she nor her husband knew anything at all about David or Doris's actions on the 16th, until they learned about them the same way everyone else in town did.

Soon, David returned to the school area, climbing Cemetery Hill to get a clearer view of the grounds. The kids were on their lunch break, many of them still outside, running around. He would have to wait. He didn't really mind. If he had waited all these years, he could wait a few more minutes.

While those minutes ticked by, David presumably went over the plan one more time in his mind. Suddenly, he put the binoculars down—the waiting was over. He returned to the van, drove down the hill, past the junction with the Smith's Fork road and across U.S. 30, over the Spring Creek Bridge and into the school yard. Nobody was there—perfect. Afternoon classes had begun. David parked at the south entrance and started giving orders. With Mendenhall and Deppe secured in the van, he had only his obedient wife and nervous daughter to help carry in all the firearms, and the bomb.

From the large arsenal he had brought, David set aside the following weaponry to be taken into the school: five rifles, including two AR-15 semi-automatics, five pistols, ample ammunition for all the above, additional ammo to be placed inside the bomb, and 30 blasting caps. These were in addition to the bomb itself with its own five blasting caps.

The three must have made quite a sight, had anyone been outside to see them, as they made their way up the walk, struggling with all the guns and wheeling the cart full of assembled bomb components. In addition, they had some of David's favorite journals, philosophical pamphlets to hand out, and of course, David's syringes and insulin for his diabetes.

David wore his pistols tucked beneath his dark blue nylon jacket, worn over an unbuttoned yellow sweater. Beneath that was a navy blue T-shirt. He was wearing faded jeans and his beard was scraggly, but he looked no more threatening or unkempt than many Cokeville men did after coming home from a hard day's cattle roundup, fence-mending or rodeo practice. Even in red T-shirt and pink pants, Doris didn't look particularly conspicuous, either.

The two of them, with Princess bringing up the rear, entered the south doorway a few minutes after 1:00 p.m. Feeling confident at having penetrated his objective, David looked around carefully at the empty corridor. He'd had no opportunity to study the floor plan of the school in advance—it had been built after his brief residence in 1977. Gesturing to Doris and Princess to come along, he rolled the deadman's bomb down the hallway that stretched silently in front of them. He knew they would meet up with somebody before long. It was time to announce his presence.

Chapter Three

A TOWN WITHOUT CHILDREN

*"There is no doubt in my mind that David Young planned to kill
the children to gain control of their minds."*
—*Ron Hartley, Sheriff's Investigator*

The end of the south hallway turned right. David and
his little group followed the turn and saw, near the
front entranceway a counter and receptionist's desk next to
the principal's office. Someone was seated at the desk.

Christina "Tina" Cook, school receptionist, looked up as
she heard someone approaching. Originally from Canada,
she had moved from Washington D.C. to Cokeville after
David's time, so she had no reason to recognize any of the
people coming down the hall, burdened with what looked
like a stack of guns and something in a shopping cart. Casual
attire and paraphernalia of one kind or another were familiar
sights to anybody living in a rural, outdoor-active town. Tina
greeted them as she would any other visitor to the school.

"Hello," she said with her usual smile. There was no
response from either Doris or Princess. The man came closer
and then stood, also silently, just watching her. She was
surprised at the grim look on his face. At almost the same
moment, another woman came up. Tina assumed she was

with the others, because she had never seen her either.

This woman, however, was Cindy Cowden, who had an appointment with school principal Max Excell. She was there to interview for a teaching position that was open in the kindergarten. Since Mr. Excell was not in sight, and the receptionist was busy with three other people, Cindy decided to step into the restroom.

Tina's attention came back to the three standing in front of her. The man was speaking. "Mrs. Cook," he said, scrutinizing her nameplate, "is that your name?"

"Yes, it is. Can I help you?" Tina tried again to initiate a normal conversation.

"You certainly can," he responded, but said nothing more.

Tina had never seen so depressing and cheerless a look as the one on his face. With a shock, she understood it was really possible for a person to have "cold eyes." The man leaned toward her.

"Mrs. Cook, this is a revolution! This school is being taken hostage!" He could see she hadn't quite taken in his announcement. "Don't push any alarms, answer any phones, or call for help! We are very serious, Mrs. Cook. I have guns and this is a bomb." David opened his jacket and pointed clearly to the shoelace-trigger attached to his wrist and its connection to the shopping cart.

Tina looked from the pile of components back to David, still in disbelief. He was explaining about the clothespin detonator.

"See where I have inserted the plug between the two ends of the pin? I have only to let them touch, Mrs. Cook, and this entire building, with everyone in it, blows sky high. Mrs. Cook, you and I are only one-half inch from death."

Tina felt a spurt of anger. She wished he would stop saying her name like that, over and over again, especially in that sepulchral tone. She hadn't moved from the mean streets of Washington D.C. to this rural haven where people raised families in love and respect, just to be threatened at her desk by a rude, self-important stranger.

David must have seen the doubt in her eyes. Even more pointedly he said, "Try to hit me on the head, jump me from behind, or anything at all, and I will pull this bomb trigger as I go down. Do I make myself clear, Mrs. Cook?"

He was making himself ridiculous, she thought, but realized he saw himself much differently than that. She couldn't even think how to respond.

"How many telephones do you have here in the school, Mrs. Cook?" he was asking.

"Five," she managed to say.

"Well, unplug them. All five." She looked at him numbly for a minute and then got up and walked to the principal's office to comply. "Stop!" he suddenly shouted. Doris came up to Tina and looked at her closely. "May I impress upon your mind, Mrs. Cook"—now she was doing it!— "that the lives of everyone in this building depend on what you do in the next several minutes?" Tina could only nod.

Just then, Cindy Cowden reappeared. She saw David

gesture to her, and said "No, I'm fine. I'll just wait for Mr. Excell right here."

"Lady, you better get over here with the others," he replied. Cindy didn't like being ordered around by this man.

Again she said, "No, I'll just wait right here." Without speaking, David lifted the barrel of his pistol and aimed it at her. She couldn't believe it. "What's this," she laughed, "a new interviewing technique?" Tina shook her head at Cindy, and the receptionist's terse expression sobered her immediately. As instructed, she joined the group.

At this moment, Janel Dayton came to the office to pick up her mail. She had been a Cokeville first-grade teacher for several years, and had six children, her youngest in the morning kindergarten. Her husband ran their family ranch north of town. She took in the entourage with a look, and decided she would just go back to her room and pick up her mail later. Before she could, David turned and once more loudly announced, "This is a revolution!"

She turned back. "Who do you represent?" she asked him.

"Ourselves!" he said. Janel tried to walk away, but he stopped her. Like Tina and Cindy, she was soon made a part of the group.

The next person to come upon the gathering was fifth-grade teacher Rocky Moore, intent on getting some papers he wanted from his desk. Suddenly he heard an angry voice. "You! Get over here with the others behind this counter!"

A stocky and determined man, not the type to be bullied,

he muttered "That'll be the day!" and merely kept on going.

"I know you, Rocky!" the voice boomed again. Moore stopped to see who was talking. As he walked back, he suddenly found himself looking down the barrel of a pistol, less than a foot away. Then the man who had spoken cocked the gun. It was so close Rocky could see the slug in firing position. "You don't remember me," David said. "But I'd just as soon kill you right now as later." He seemed really angry. "Get over here and keep quiet!"

Rocky shrugged his shoulders. "Okay. Hey, I'm coming, if that's the way you feel about it." He knew the tall man now. David had been his tenant years ago. There had been the usual disagreements about repairs and rent paid on time. David wanted more than repairs; he wanted remodeling. Rocky had told him he was free to leave. He thought little more about the man once David moved away. But David didn't forget him. He didn't like not getting his way. That wasn't the way things should be.

Rocky realized that confronting David now would only make matters worse. Since the man already bore him a grudge, Rocky decided to stay as quiet and inconspicuous as possible and wait the turn of events. David already seemed to have forgotten him anyway, and was concentrating on looking for a bigger space to commandeer. He shepherded everyone toward the adjacent conference room. "Is that a large room?" he asked.

"No, it isn't," Tina said. Cindy Cowden and Janel Dayton were pushed right into the room as David kept the group together while he looked inside.

Cindy noticed an open window. She suggested to Janel that they climb out and run. Janel thought about it seriously. But she had just turned over her first-grade class to fellow-teacher Jean Mitchell for combined activities with Mrs. Mitchell's students. It was the first day of their trade arrangement, and both teachers were excited about the approach. Janel considered what might happen if the man found out she was missing and decided to take it out on Jean or any of the children. No, she decided, she would have to stay and see the whole thing through.

While David was looking over the accommodations, Princess was sent to the van to bring in more weapons. By the time she returned, a newcomer had joined the group, 66-year-old teacher's aide Verlene Bennion. It was clear that the conference room would not be big enough for the number of people David intended to capture—many more than those taken hostage so far. Once everyone realized that the shopping cart held a genuine bomb and that he was ready to detonate it if crossed, it wasn't hard to herd them back down the south hallway, looking for the most appropriate room.

There are unanswered questions about what happened next. Tina Cook thought Princess was an enthusiastic conspirator, as guilty as David and Doris of planning and executing the takeover of the school. Others felt her actions at this point showed that she was coerced into helping and had no wish to harm anyone. Whatever her state of mind at the moment, she appears to have come to some kind of breaking point. Several of the group heard her say to David "My God! My God! I can't believe you would do this to innocent children!" Then she simply turned and walked away.

David's reaction to this outburst is almost impossible to define. Hindsight suggests he could easily have lost control, ordering Princess to remain, and if further crossed, attacking her or one of the innocent bystanders, perhaps even setting off the bomb. Perhaps she would have given in and obeyed his orders if he had simply cowed her with verbal threats. But also, perhaps, he saw something in his daughter's face that no one else could, and knew she was more dangerous to his plans if she stayed than if she left. Whatever the case, witnesses all agree that he tossed the van keys to her and shouted "Take these then, and get the hell out of here!" She left the building immediately, taking with her David and Doris's only avenue of escape.

Quickly reasserting his authority after Princess's defection, David settled on the middle door of the hallway and told Doris to go round up the other children and bring them all to him. He stood at the entrance to Room 4, where Mrs. Mitchell was presenting a flannel-board story to the combined class of her students and Janel Dayton's. After she finished "Goldilocks and the Three Bears," Jean Mitchell intended to move smoothly into a discussion of magnets and then into the kids' favorite discussion topic, dinosaurs. Later, they would practice arithmetic and spelling. The afternoon was well-planned and the students seemed to be enjoying the story.

She was therefore a little irritated when a shaggy-looking man barged into her room, pulling a cart and surrounded by a group of people, some of whom she knew and some she had never seen before. She was even more surprised when the man began stacking rifles against her classroom wall. She soon realized he had pistols tucked in his belt as well. Before she could adjust to the invasion, he was inside the room, as were the five other people with him, and he was sounding very much in charge.

Within a few minutes, a crowd of other students began streaming through her door, taking the papers being handed out to them by a woman Jean didn't know, but who was obviously with the bearded man. Doris had managed her task very well. Thinking her invitation to be on the orders of Principal Max Excell, several of the teachers she had confronted had willingly led their students behind her along to Room 4. Music teacher John Miller had been swept along with them. In minutes, Jean's room, designed for 30, held 135 children and 18 adults.

Ten-year-old Jerry Dayton was curious about what was going on. The lady had told his class "Follow me! ... I have a surprise for you!" When he got in the room and saw all the guns and the strange people, he remembered they had been studying Libya recently. Maybe the school had put together a kind of assembly to teach everybody how to defend themselves against terrorists. It was a neat idea.

The room David selected was good for his purposes.

There was no door to the outside and the window sections that were movable were small, only opening part way. More and more self-assured as growing numbers of school children came under his gaze, David watched Doris hand out more of his pamphlets and waited for the commotion to die down.

Jean Mitchell wasn't ready to relinquish her classroom. "You've got to be kidding!" she said. David scowled. "This is MY room!" she pressed.

David wouldn't condescend to argue. "Sit down and shut up!" he told her, and there was no mistaking the threat— "or else" had been clearly implied.

Others were still being dragged into the situation. The special education teacher, Gloria Mower, was working one-on-one with a student in the adjoining room when the commotion began to distract her. Peeking into Room 4, she and her student were "invited" in. Fourth-grade teacher Kliss Sparks, as much like a grandmother to her students as their instructor, was treating the class to an outdoor session on the lawn, the perfect place to read out loud from *Tom Sawyer.* Hearing the noise inside, however, she thought perhaps she had missed word of a program of some kind intended for her students as well. She took the class in, and found herself trapped with everyone else. Now she struggled to forgive herself for exposing her students to danger.

Sandy Gonzales, a UPS driver, came down the hall looking for someone to accept her delivery. Soon, she was one of the hostages. Eva Clark, who had earlier called the school not to be worried about Paul being a bit late, had just arrived with him and was taking him to class. Her four-year-old, Kathy, was left in the car, since Eva would be right back. Arriving at Paul's classroom, she was surprised to find it empty. The library was vacant as well. Then she saw teacher Jack Mitchell coming down the hall. "They might be down in my wife's room," Jack told her with a laugh. "It looks like they've got something going on down there. Jean is always cooking up something new."

Eva and Paul went to Room 4, where the boy quickly found his classmates. The woman at the door beckoned Eva in as well. Intent on her afternoon tasks, Eva barely noticed her. Spring branding was scheduled to begin the next day, and she had shopping to do in Montpelier before she could even begin to help her husband Lowell bring the cattle in. Lots of relatives were coming, some from out of state. To host them properly, and complete all the preparations, she would have to stick to her list.

"I've got to go," Eva smiled at the woman who had gestured to her.

"No, come in," the woman said. "You'll want to see this."

"I just haven't got the time," Eva tried to explain. Again, the woman insisted. This time her expression was irritable rather than smiling.

Then Janel Dayton came up. "You may want to stay," she said quietly. "We have a problem here." Suddenly Eva thought about the five of her six children who were in the room. She saw the pistols David was wearing and the shoelace-trigger attached to his wrist. There was no question.

She would have to stay.

School Custodian Delbert Rentfro had not yet been seen by either David or Doris. He met up with Principal Max Excell and told him that the fifth graders were in their classroom but that their teacher, Mr. Miller wasn't there. "The kids are starting to get a bit noisy," he said. Since it was very unlike Mr. Miller, a much-respected music teacher on loan from the high school, to be tardy or absent without notice, Excell went to look for him. On the way, he observed the milling and confusion around Room 4. What he saw in the doorway made him even more concerned—an unauthorized assembly—an assembly, in fact, of most of the school, crammed together in one classroom! He spotted John Miller about the same time he realized something was very wrong. "What is going on here?" he demanded.

David knew an authority figure when he saw one. "Are you the principal?" he asked. Excell said yes, and repeated his question. Getting no satisfactory answer, Excell sat down and studied the children. Many of them were attempting to play or read. He noticed they also frequently looked up at David and Doris as if hoping they would be gone the next time they looked. The children were apparently very aware of the cart and its importance, and realized that David was consciously holding his hand low and quiet.

"I didn't get the feeling he was acting," said one child later. "He was too careful to keep his hand down all the time."

One of his friends explained, "A teacher told me that we

needed to be quiet and not upset the man. One jerk from his wrist and the bomb would blow. I kept watching to see that he kept his wrist down."

Excell realized that there were things they needed to have in the room if the adults were going to keep the children well and occupied. He asked David for permission to gather up boxes of tissue, aspirin and other things needed to keep the children settled down. David told him he could have a few minutes, and the principal went out to forage.

When he came back, he learned that David had more plans for him. He named Excell his spokesman and told the principal to call authorities and state that he wanted $2 million for each of the kids. "I want no part of the negotiations," said David. "They have a way of trying to break you down. I don't want to waste time with that. You do the talking."

Excell tried to keep his voice calm. Over a hundred kids meant over two hundred million dollars, just as a ball-park figure. What realistic hopes of getting that large a ransom even existed? But he couldn't solve that part of it now. "Who do you want me to call first?" he asked David. "The sheriff?"

"That's fine," David replied benignly, and then continued, "Tell them I'm prepared to be here 10 days or more if necessary. It may take Congress that long to raise the money."

Excell thought the man was calm enough to risk a question. "Why this school," he asked, keeping his voice very low. "Why here?"

David was very willing to reply. "Because this is a family town," he said, "where people love their children, and they'll do anything to get them back." Unknown to Excell and the others, David was not just guessing. Later investigations proved that he had taken notes while living in Cokeville about the school children and their families, including such things as who was close friends with whom. David's answer to Excell was thus much more than a casual remark. In fact, it was a real conclusion David had drawn about the kind of people who inhabited this small, but in his eyes unique, western town.

As Excell got up to make his first outside call, David gave him a sharp warning. "Be back here every ten minutes to make your report—or I'll start shooting these kids one by one." Later, probably recognizing the impractical constraint he was placing on Excell, David allowed 15 minutes instead of ten.

Excell left for his office to make the all-important call. He tried to compute the total dollar amount of David's ransom demand. It would be staggering. And probably impossible to get. Inside his office, he called the sheriff's office and told them what was happening. He was surprised to learn they had just been contacted by someone else, a young woman calling herself Princess who had made a "strange report" about a "hostage crisis" at the elementary school. Excell quickly confirmed her story. "It's happening to us. Right now!" he assured the sheriff's secretary.

Princess had indeed used her unexpected freedom, not

to disappear into safe anonymity, but to go for help. With Deppe and Mendenhall still shackled in the van, she swiftly drove to the town hall, two blocks west, and burst hysterically through the first door she saw, confronting a startled clerk. "Is there a police officer here?" she demanded.

Nadine Dana said there was not. "Maybe I can help you," she offered. No, Princess wanted a policeman. Nadine said she thought she could handle it.

Frustrated, Princess poured out her incredible tale. She was excited, difficult to understand, sometimes rambling and sometimes profane. The noise brought city employee Kevin Walker over, where he took the stranger aside. "We don't talk like that around here," he admonished her.

"Don't you folks care about your children?" Princess demanded. She looked back and forth at the two city workers and tried to order her thoughts so she could communicate with them. "My father has a bomb, and he is going to blow up the grade school!" Mrs. Dana felt sick. She had twin daughters in third grade, Joella and Ranella, and she knew all the other children as well. Kevin Walker had three children, Travis, Kathy and Rachel. From his expression, it was clear Kevin also realized that, whoever the woman was, she was totally serious.

Across the hall, an emergency-strategy meeting was just breaking up. Wyoming regional watermaster John Teichert, Civil Defense and U.S. Army Corp of Engineers officials were discussing a flood which was threatening northside residents along Smiths Fork. Having decided on the appropriate emergency measures, the corpsmen had already left for their homes. Teichert, who lived in Cokeville, and the Civil Defense workers who, like the corpsmen, all lived in other parts of the state, were just about to leave.

They came out of their meeting to the news that the elementary school was under siege. The urgency of the flood suddenly vanished. Teichert was not only the regional watermaster, but a lifelong resident of the town and a local Mormon bishop. A number of the students were in his congregation; he knew most of the kids in town by name.

As the scope and danger of their problem became clear to him, his first impulse was to pray. Seeking out a private room downstairs, Teichert pleaded for the Lord to intervene in some way for the sake of the children. "I emphasized how every child in there was vital to this community," Teichert said. "I told God we would do all we could, but we would need His help."

The Civil Defense workers, Kathy Davison, Bob Looney and Grant Sorensen, immediately began making emergency contacts. Davison had been a sheriff's dispatcher, so she had considerable experience obtaining the needed help. With the aid of Mrs. Dana, they alerted ambulances in Cokeville and in Lincoln County, at the county seat of Kemmerer and also at Afton, both communities about 50 miles away. Davison then tried to locate the four law enforcement officers who lived in Cokeville. Through luck or prior planning on David's part, the four were all out of town. Sheriff's Deputy Ron Hartley was on his day off, as was local Police Chief Cal

Fredrickson. Wyoming Highway Patrolman Brad Anderson was located via radio near Kemmerer where he was patrolling. Sheriff's Deputy Earl Carroll lived in Cokeville, but was working in Kemmerer as well that day. He was the first lawman to reach the town hall.

By the time Deputy Carroll arrived, Max Excell's first contact with the sheriff's department had been made. The authorities learned quickly that they had better not let themselves be seen near the school building. David had promised, through Excell, that he would start shooting if anyone appeared. Princess confirmed that her father was fully capable of doing just that. Warnings to keep their distance from the school were relayed to each new official, as he or she arrived. Officer Carroll understood what Principal Excell was trying to tell him. "You're there and we aren't," he told Excell. "We'll take our cues from you. But...damn!"

Even with this warning, it was imperative to get close enough to the school to make some kind of informed analysis about the situation there. The new building grounds were almost bare; there was just flat lawn all the way to the fence. Part of the boundary abutted Art Robinson's back yard. Eventually officers tried to see into Room 4 using binoculars from a position behind Art's fence. Officers risked being easily seen if they moved while someone was looking out the window. But the officers themselves could only see, through the narrow, horizontal windows, vague figures moving about. It wasn't very helpful.

During the interval after Deputy Carroll was located and

before he arrived, Princess found the key to the handcuffs, finally allowing Deppe and Mendenhall to be released. Princess's description of the morning of the takeover had basically exonerated them, but all three were, in effect, detained so that they could provide as much information as possible. John Teichert volunteered to keep an eye on them until Carroll and more deputies arrived. Deppe and Mendenhall were then questioned to glean every possible detail about David Young and his scheme.

Princess's information was particularly alarming. She described the number and kind of weapons she had helped carry into the school and the kind of bomb David was using. It was now clear that the takeover was a true case of terrorism. When Deputy Carroll arrived, he remained at the town hall to coordinate emergency operations. Officer Davison and others alerted the Sweetwater County Sheriff's Office, including bomb expert Rich Haskell; Teton County's SWAT Team; Bear Lake County, Idaho's Sheriff Brent Bunn and his deputies, and men from the Sheriff's Department in Rich County, Utah. Neighboring counties also promised help, if needed.

Since hostage-taking had been made a federal offense in 1932, result of the Lindbergh kidnapping, federal agencies also came onto the case—the F.B.I.'s primary jurisdiction was the hostage-taking aspect of the case, while the Bureau of Alcohol, Tobacco, and Firearms was particularly interested in the aspect of weapons violations.

Everyone in Cokeville who had an official responsibility

was mobilized; every EMT and firefighter was suddenly on call. The takeover crisis was the very first call for new EMT Glenna Walker, and one of the first for her husband Kevin, who was already somewhat informed from talking to Princess at the town hall. They had the best reasons for wanting to help: their three children in the school.

The growing official response held an irony few recognized at the time. One reason David had chosen Cokeville, apparently, was that he "didn't want lawmen or others swooping down on him to thwart his plans." But in this part of the sparsely populated, rural West, deadly attacks on one community were quickly seen as attacks against the whole region. Response to the small town's plight was probably as swift and complete as it would have been in an ultra-modern, technology-driven, big-city emergency. "Strange he should select a rural area as safer for him than a city metropolis," one observer remarked. "In the latter, he could vanish far more easily into a jungle of buildings and hideouts. Here a helicopter or vehicles could have easily followed him in the wide open spaces."

As the long arm of the law began to curl around Cokeville, word of the takeover began to spread through the town itself. Some fathers pondered whether to unlock big game rifles from their gun cabinets and drive to the school. Some mothers rushed to the police lines set up around the schoolyard; some stayed away, not sure whether their presence would help or hurt. Radio broadcasters Ken Rand of Kemmerer's KMER and Robin Spurling of Afton's KRSV began covering the situation.

High school principal Dale Lamborn had the unpleasant task of notifying students of the intense situation under way. He asked the students to stay away from the hostage scene, even though many had younger brothers and sisters in the building. A number of the senior high students were teacher's aides at the elementary school. Senior high classmates expressed their feelings to each other, and especially to fellow students like Danny and Billy Mitchell. Their younger brother Chad was a hostage. But so were both of their parents, Jack and Jean.

Teacher's aide/high school student Cindy Wixom first learned what had happened when her teacher, Richard Pieper, a volunteer fireman, was called out of class. Custodian Bob Dayton came in to sit with the students and explained the matter bluntly: "He's got the kids and he's got the bomb." Cindy's brother Kamron was one of the kids.

Before school dismissed, many of the senior high students gathered in the auditorium for a prayer. Principal Dale Lamborn pleaded for divine guidance. Later, students recalled that they and their teachers had been spiritually united as never before. Many wept openly, unashamed to share their deepest feelings of fear and love with classmates and leaders.

"All this and no one even consulted the American Civil Liberties Union," a sophomore remarked. "Well, the ACLU can go hang its head," another student said. "Those are my friends in there, and I want to do everything possible, and I mean everything possible, to get them out alive."

While the reality of the takeover was being communicated throughout town, in the school building itself, Custodian Delbert Rentfro was still trying to figure out what was happening in Room 4. Shortly after Max Excell was on his way to make the first contact with the sheriff's office, Delbert approached the door of the classroom and looked inside. Doris, who was still at the door, apparently decided that Rentfro should be excluded from the hostage group. It is not known why she did this, unless it was simply the fact that Rentfro, at 6 ft. 3 inches and 225 pounds, was the one hostage they might not be able to control. "Forget it," she said, closing him out almost abruptly. He thought her rude, but left for the kitchen, where he had some work to do.

David Young took this time to lay some ground rules. Certain teachers were told to stay away from the area around the door, while Janel Dayton was appointed door monitor. She was instructed to allow no one out. The children were not to use the drinking fountain in the room. "If you drink too much you'll have to use the bathroom," David said. And he didn't want them in the bathroom either, even though it was accessible directly from Room 4. "The man does not know children," Mrs. Dayton thought to herself. "Forbidding nervous children from using a bathroom—how will this ever turn out?"

Doris tried to give the children some practical advice. "Wet some tissue paper and hold it to your face." But this, of course, couldn't work, since the children were not allowed to approach the fountain to wet the tissue. Teachers could see that the youngsters were getting confused about what they should and shouldn't do. They turned to combining their efforts in hopes of finding pragmatic solutions to the growing problem. Some handed out nearby books while others asked permission to gather those from farther shelves. David nodded. He seemed to want the children to behave as much as the teachers did.

Eva Clark was still reacting to the reality of being a hostage. With most of her children hostages as well, and the tensions and needs of the immediate situation taking precedence, she had completely forgotten that her four-year-old Kathy was still out in the car, waiting for her mother to return from bringing young Paul into school. Eva almost panicked. She approached Doris immediately, trying to explain the problem. "I've got to get out to that car and get my young daughter!" she pleaded.

"You aren't going anywhere!" Doris replied.

Eva was desperate. "Please let me go out and get my baby. I'll bring her right in here with me."

Doris wasn't willing to trust that Eva would return. "You'll stay right here," she repeated with more irritation. She didn't look to David for confirmation; he seemed to know but be disinterested in the outcome.

Eva tried a new approach. "I'll stay here," she agreed. "But can someone else go out and get her?" She suggested Christy or Elizabeth, two of her older children in the room. There was still no positive response. Eva tried one last idea.

"How about you getting her then?"

This produced a complete change. Doris immediately said "Sure, I'll get her," even sounding pleased about the errand. She went out without delay and returned quickly with Kathy, who seemed little ruffled considering her somewhat long and lonely wait.

"The lady was nice to me," she told her mother cheerfully.

Max Excell had returned from his first phone calls and had made his report to David, who accepted what he was told with no display of emotion. Excell was mildly surprised. Before long, David demanded of each teacher a head count of their particular students. He added the figures they gave him so swiftly in his head that the hostages were amazed.

Noting their students growing more restless, teachers asked for permission to gather crayons and coloring books and more reading material, anything that might help them keep the children occupied. These requests were granted, with the usual stern warning: "Don't forget to come back, or you know what will happen to the children." When the materials were assembled, teachers realized that they had too few books for the smallest children. They had to ask David for permission to go out again. He was silent, merely gesturing approval. But his eyes told them he had marked in his mind how long they were gone.

Second-grade teacher Carol Petersen helped distribute story books and then moved near the door to be with some of her students. She suddenly realized David was watching her closely. She didn't understand why she had caught his attention, but he was definitely studying her. She felt even more exposed when he beckoned her to approach. Perhaps, she thought, she was going to be the first one to die. Why else would he make her stand in front of him? She slowly walked toward him and stopped. But now, he was totally ignoring her! She didn't know what to do. Perhaps he had simply wanted her to move away from the door. Quietly, she found a seat somewhere else.

At one point, David made a statement which referred directly to the situation, but not in words that were easy to interpret. He said, in almost a sympathetic tone, "Children are precious. We don't want to hurt them. I'll only shoot the kids with a .22."

With his ground rules announced, David launched into a formal statement of his beliefs. Sitting on a stool he began "I'm the most wanted man in this culture.... The government and your teachers are polluting your minds. We're going to get some money and...." It was difficult even for those sitting closest to him to hear what he said. They did catch a bit more. "I've got these papers here I've handed to the teachers. They tell you about my philosophy. You will learn later what we have in mind for you." And that was all.

The adults had hoped to keep him talking. He might say something that would help them understand how to defuse the situation. But he was silent and sullen again. It was about 1:45 p.m.—from then on, Doris did most of the talking. David seemed at times smug, at other times merely bored. He limited his reactions to raising his wrist slightly but ominously, if he didn't like something he saw.

Shortly after his speech, David pulled the bomb cart about, not sure where he wanted to place it for maximum surveillance of the 30' x 30' room. Finally, he pulled up a child's desk and leaned on it. This seemed to satisfy him. As he settled down, and turned his gaze back on the occupants, his look had the tiresome scrutiny of one obliged to duty.

But to the children, it seemed more malevolent. "He looked mean, as if to keep us frightened," one of the kids said. "And he did."

2:00 p.m. Jack Mitchell began to notice how difficult it was to breathe. It was more than stuffy in the crowded room—something smelled like gasoline! Jack took a careful look at the bomb cart and realized that the gasoline jug was leaking. Very slowly, but leaking. Even as he realized what the problem was, one of the girls got up with a hand over her mouth and ran for the sink. The fumes were clearly making the children nauseated. Not long after, another student threw up in a wastebasket. Neither dared ask David for permission to go to the bathroom. The children were not only frightened of him; now they were becoming ill. Something had to be done.

Jean Mitchell approached David and asked permission to air out the room by opening the windows and doors. David agreed on the condition that a table barricade be set up across the door nearest the bathroom, which was out of his line of sight, as he sat facing the center of the room. The windows were too small to become escape routes—the door was his main concern. The barricade was set up, allowing easy access into the restroom, but not beyond into the hallway. Mrs. Dayton was ordered to sit by the door and prevent any child from going through it. At one point she noticed one small boy eyeing the barricade at close range. When he began to climb through, she had to tell him to come back. She hated having to help David Young keep this youngster imprisoned.

Opening the windows and doors had made the atmosphere more bearable, but it had also made Doris nervous about the children going near the glass. She alluded to having accomplices at the hallway doors, and made hints that snipers were outside, waiting to shoot anyone who got too close to the windows. The children knew these threats could easily be true.

Teachers noted that some of the children were gathered in groups with their heads bowed. "Let's have a prayer. Pass it on," one of Jack Mitchell's sixth graders said. The 12-year-olds asked Allyson Cornia to voice a prayer for their group. "Father in Heaven, help us, please help us if the bomb goes off...."

"Do you think our Father-in-Heaven would let us all die?" one boy asked. "No!" said another positively. If David noticed any of these prayers, he said nothing about them. The man who had written that God exists only in man's mind was little concerned if the hostages prayed for deliverance.

2:15 p.m. The children seemed to be having troubles

again. Some of those who hadn't shown any fear were now looking shocked and scared. Some moved around aimlessly, looking for something to do, and risking becoming a nuisance to David. Some of the children were still reacting creatively—making up mock television scenarios about how they would emerge triumphant. They whispered these to each other when they were far enough away from David. Looking at him only made them frightened again. Several children told Doris that they had a headache. Her solution was simple. "Now, listen children," she told them. "Just don't think about it anymore." That was that.

2:30 p.m. Jean Mitchell watched the children wriggle with discomfort in the overcrowded room. One child moved a neighbor's leg which had strayed over his own. The owner put it back. There was a small battle of wills with the children frowning at each other. Jean glanced at the man sitting so quietly by his bomb. He was watching the tiff with complete detachment. Jean wondered what would happen when he stopped being detached.

Suddenly she remembered that the dismissal bells would ring in little over an hour. They would signal the children to go home. At 3:25 p.m., would anyone be able to hold them back? Just by instinct, they would try to run out the door, all at once, and then....

Her husband Jack was talking to the older kids. Like his wife, he had noticed the little ones were having a difficult time. "No one asked for what is happening to us today," he told his sixth-graders. "You are the oldest students. We need you to be brave! We all feel fear here, but for awhile, we must not show it. I'm counting on you. I know you can do it."

Rocky Moore chimed in, "That's right, kids," he whispered. "I know you can do it, too."

The 12-year-olds thought they were old enough to help. They circulated quietly from one little one to the next, smiling, giving a pat on the back, telling them they would get out of this somehow. Jack and Rocky proudly watched their kids respond to the challenge. It tore Jack up to see them under such stress, however well they were facing it. Suddenly, he felt a surge of energy. He could hold back his feelings no longer. "We've got to get the children out of here! We'll have them out by 4:00 p.m.!"

David's reaction was immediate. He jerked his hand down to the gun in his belt, then suddenly stopped. Jack sat down, horrified at what he had almost set off. Jean, just as terrified, saw the anger slowly drain from David's face. Her boy Chad, sitting nearby, gave his mother a fierce hug. She felt both agony and relief in his embrace. Why, why did David have to put the children through this?

As Jack thought about what had just happened, he realized with complete clarity that he and the other teachers were powerless. "There is absolutely nothing any mortal can do," he said to himself. "We are utterly helpless. Even if we stormed the man, he could shoot a child or explode the bomb as he falls down."

Doris was approaching Jack, carrying something in her hand. She had found an EMT radio in another room, and now she asked him to show her how to use it. Jack, a licensed ham radio operator, knew very well, but wasn't going to help her. He said he didn't know how to use it. Doris, however, experimented with the dials, and managed to find the police channel herself. She was soon listening to every stratagem the authorities were at that moment discussing outside the building. She even heard Patrolman Brad Anderson report to the town hall that he had set up a command post where he could look down the school's south hallway from a Main Street back yard.

Principal Excell was out on one of his telephone contact runs for David. As soon as he returned, Jack quietly motioned him over. "Tell the police to get off the radio! They'll have to communicate some other way. These people can hear everything they're saying outside." When Excell went out for his next call, he reported the problem. Within a few minutes, the police channel went dead. The small psychological victory gave the teachers fresh hope.

As Excell was on his way to make that call, Delbert Rentfro was on his way back from the kitchen, still uncertain about the goings-on in Room 4. Now he heard the telephone ringing repeatedly, with no one answering. As he came down the hall, he saw Excell hurrying toward his office. "Delbert!" exclaimed the principal. "We're all being held hostage in Mrs. Mitchell's room. Get over to the town hall while you can. Tell them to be sure they keep everyone away from the school building! We can't risk anyone trying to get in."

The custodian hurried out of the building, found no one

barring his way, and ran to the town hall. There he relayed his boss's message, giving lawmen a good description of the Youngs and their location in the school, and updating the initial information Princess had given. After giving his report, he suddenly felt very strange. He almost wished he was inside that room with the kids. He felt separated and horribly frustrated, not knowing what was happening to them.

Many other people felt as he did. The high school track team, competing at Casper, Wyoming in a regional meet, was notified of the crisis. "We had no more heart to do anything but finish up quickly and get home," one athlete said. "Our brothers and sisters were in that school. I think others did as I did. They prayed; then they prayed again," another student commented.

The senior civics class was taking a tour of Utah's Point-of-the-Mountain Prison just south of Salt Lake City. One of the students, Andra Birch, remarked that she would "be glad to get back to Cokeville where I didn't have to think about problems with crime and criminals." When she arrived home, she learned her little brother was one of those being held hostage by a man with an arsenal and a bomb.

2:45 p.m. Jean quietly flagged her husband's attention. She reminded him about the dismissal bells—they needed to be switched off soon. Jack approached David and asked for permission to leave. David studied him for a minute, then voiced no opposition. He didn't concern himself now about anyone returning. They knew the result if they didn't. Jack rushed to Tina's office and easily located the switch. He was back so quickly it seemed too brief for such a vital task. "It's done," he told his wife.

Almost 3:00 p.m. Teachers and older students watched two of the younger ones quarrel over the "funnest toys." One grabbed another boy's construction block. Music teacher John Miller was keeping his eyes open for any change in the air. Gloria Mower and media aide Gayle Chadwick were both grateful nothing had happened to trigger the bomb yet, but they wondered how much longer the standoff could go on.

Seven-year-old Jay Metcalf didn't understand what was happening—all this strange talk, the strange man with the strange look and the strange behavior. He felt strange himself. Quiet tears started to roll down his cheeks. Doris handed him a tissue.

Cindy Cowden watched what was going on around her and decided that if she and the children lived, she wanted to come here to work. "I loved these children for their determination to make the best of their circumstances. They wanted to do what their teachers told them. I fell in love with them," Cindy said. Several children near her again began to pray. She held their hands and prayed with them. "They haven't given up hope," she thought. "Neither can I."

Suddenly Jeremiah Moore remembered it was his birthday. David was asked: could they sing "Happy Birthday"? Surprisingly, not only did David agree, but he and Doris joined in half-heartedly. As the music seemed to have a settling influence on the children, David allowed other songs to be sung. Kliss Sparks stood up to lead, and for several precious minutes, some of the smaller children almost forgot where they were and why.

After the sing-in, Jack Mitchell watched as the reinvigorated kids began to wander dangerously close to David and the bomb cart. David even gestured to clear the kids away. From the nearest desk, Jack took some masking tape. Quickly, he taped off what he told the children was a "magic square." The forbidden area left a wide berth around David and his cart. "Don't go across this line!" Jack told the children. "If you do, you're out of the game!" He was relieved to see the gap widen between David and the kids.

Some of the children held an almost congenial conversation with Doris. Drew Cornia wanted to know how long they would be there. When Doris told him ten days or more, he paused. "If you're going to hold us here ten days, I hope you brought us some toothbrushes."

"I hadn't considered that," Doris said with the trace of a smile.

3:05 p.m. Suddenly, David felt too warm. He decided to remove his jacket and sweater, even though it required lifting the same wrist with the shoelace trigger. Everyone in the room stopped still, mesmerized as they watched David pull his sleeve down to the shoelace. At one point, he seemed stuck. Doris assisted him, and he finally got the garment peeled down to the wrist, where he let it stay. "I could not hear anyone breathing," Kam Wixom said. "It was as if we had turned to statues. We didn't dare do anything until he quit moving his wrist around."

At times, David seemed to show signs of confusion. At other moments, he still seemed smug. "People pay attention when you're holding elementary school children," he gloated to Excell.

Excell mentioned two students to David, one who had epilepsy and one who had diabetes. David approved of having a doctor come to the school. But he would not consider letting the diabetic boy go unless he was replaced by two older hostages. Excell let the matter drop.

Kliss Sparks also noticed David's erratic behavior. She asked for permission to visit the library again to get more books for the children. It was readily given. "But if you don't come back, one of these kids is going to die," David told her suddenly and sharply. His voice was much more menacing than before.

3:10 p.m. The children were running out of coloring book pages. Jean asked permission to leave "just to make copies on the machine in the faculty room." David granted permission. But when Jean got there, she realized the machine had been off for two hours, and would now take at least four minutes just to warm up. She knelt down and prayed fervently while waiting for the minutes to pass. "We've tried everything! Please help the children do what we cannot do for them." Getting up to make her copies, she felt better for admitting how tense she had become through the endless afternoon.

On returning to Room 4, Jean felt David's eyes on her and knew he had noted the delay. She passed out the papers and tried to get the youngsters involved as quickly and quietly as she could. During her absence, Jack and student teacher Kris Kasper has been given time to bring a television set from the media center to Room 4. A crowd of children, particularly the little ones, clamored eagerly for cartoons. "Transformers," a big favorite, came on, and the children watched, engrossed, as the cartoon creatures changed from one form to another, endlessly making war on each other. Travis Walker watched their fascination with the big bangs and shoot-outs on the screen. "Hollywood explosions don't hurt anyone," he said.

3:20 p.m. For some reason Travis felt compelled to leave his friends and go across the room to his sisters. After talking with them briefly, he rejoined his pals. Some of the children were beginning to wander aimlessly about. David saw them, but did not threaten them as before.

3:30 p.m. Jean Mitchell grew nervous. Had someone warned the bus drivers not to come by? What would the kids do if they heard the buses? Had Excell gotten word to the drivers? She wanted to call to him and ask but didn't dare.

3:35 p.m. Several teachers sensed the atmosphere begin to change. "Something was about to happen," Jean Mitchell recalled later. "You could feel the unbearable tension mounting." Eva Clark was aware of the same thing. She looked at the man with the guns and the bomb. His confidence was ebbing! Something strange was occurring— she could feel it, but she couldn't pin down what it was.

3:45 p.m. Unexpectedly, David called Doris over. He

wanted to go to the bathroom. Everyone watched quietly while he changed the shoelace-trigger from his wrist to hers. No one had heard him say anything to Doris about the bomb, and he didn't say anything now. Leaving her in his place, David walked past Jean Mitchell toward the bathroom. Jean knew the room had child-sized fixtures. "You'll just die when you see the inside," she said. David didn't find the remark amusing. He stepped inside and shut the door.

Once David was out of sight, the children relaxed. But with the removal of the tension he generated, they immediately became more restless and noisy as well. "Children!" said Jean Mitchell, "We need 'Quiet Time.'" In the mounting hubbub, she was beginning to feel ill. David had not reappeared and Jean did not want him suddenly walking out into even the semblance of disorder and confusion. Raising her hand to her head, she admitted to Doris, "I've got a headache."

"So do I," said Doris, and made the same gesture. It was the hand to which the trigger was tied.

In an instant, a huge ball of orange flame cracked into being with a deafening roar from wall to wall. Within a moment, everyone was blinded by choking black smoke. Jean Mitchell felt herself lifted up by the blast wave and thrown toward the door. The deadman's bomb had blown.

Chapter Four

"MORE THAN A MIRACLE"

"To say it was a miracle would be the understatement of the century."

—*Richard Haskell, bomb expert*

"We're all dead!" Tina Cook cried out as the room exploded around her. Bursting lights snapped out in a wave of searing heat and unbearable pressure. Eva Clark, tossed from her chair, saw Doris Young, dreadfully illuminated against the pitch-black smoke, engulfed by the fireball she had just unleashed. In the hellish pandemonium, with the clang of fire alarms suddenly beating on her eardrums, Eva felt like she was inside a sonic boom. She had never known fear like this.

Everywhere, children screamed in pain and panic. Everyone who could run or walk did so, while those who couldn't crawled or blindly groped, searching for air, for the closest way out. "Run!" boomed Jack Mitchell's voice in the half-dark of smoke and burning debris. "Get out of here! RUN!" Jack knew David Young might still be unharmed, waiting to shoot down the children and adults who had endured the tension better than he.

Janel Dayton struggled to get her bearings. She saw the

fire, the smoke, the chaos surrounding her, yet everything was utterly still. She realized she couldn't hear anything at all. In the silence, she remembered she had been guarding the south barricade, as David Young had ordered. Immediately she began to dismantle the pile of furniture, to clear a path for the children.

The smoke rolled away momentarily, and she looked back into the room. Jean Mitchell was lying on the floor not far away, alive but finding it difficult to move. Janel ran to her aid. She pulled at Jean as Jean tried to stand, but neither had enough strength. Suddenly smoke more thick and acrid than before rolled over them. Janel couldn't breathe. Choking, forced to abandon Jean, she plunged through the south door into the hallway, then up to the other door, hoping to find her first-graders.

The deafening explosion seemed to leave Carol Petersen numb. She had been sitting on the floor with kids curled across her lap. When they were swept away by the force of the explosion she tried to stand, but her muscles wouldn't respond. Terrified, she suddenly felt ridiculous as well. Was she going to die here because her legs had fallen asleep?

In the southeast corner, a great shower of flame descended on a large group of kindergartners and first-graders, who were intently watching TV. Children screamed in pain and fright as their clothes and hair caught fire. Some tried to escape from the deadly location; others attempted to beat out the flames with their bare hands.

Few knew it at the time, but the design of this deadman's

bomb sent most of its violence thrusting up to the ceiling, once the device was set off. From there the force powered out to the walls, and plummeted straight down their sides. Anyone sitting or standing near those walls would take the explosion's hottest and heaviest impact.

In contrast, children standing near the border that marked the "magic square" took the first brunt of the detonation. It seemed to Christy Clark that her skin itself was on fire. Kam Wixom and Travis Walker were luckier. They were near the doorway as the bomb went off and suddenly found themselves thrust into the hallway to safety. Tina Morfeld, further inside the room, caught a billow of super-heated air. Unable to see where to run, she had to take a breath. Instantly, the biting heat scorched her throat and lungs.

Billie Jo Hutchinson was also near the magic square, or "line of death," as the older children secretly dubbed it. Before she could move, she was hit by a wall of fire. Shocked and numbed by the blast, at first she felt no pain. All around her, teachers were probing for bodies, hoping to feel life in the small arms and legs they grasped or hear the muffled call of a child, injured but alive, still strong enough to cry for help.

Rocky Moore was near the windows. Instantly, he grabbed the first kids he saw and began stuffing them through the ten-inch-wide opening of the small ventilation window. He was amazed at how fast they went through. But the children, still dazed, some in shock, were slow to run. "I looked out and saw them stacking up like a cord of firewood," Rocky said. Still not sure whether David Young was nearby, he screamed at the kids, "Run! Run! Get away from the building!" They ran as hard as they could, then suddenly stopped at the edge of the lawn, just as in school fire drill, where they'd been taught to wait for their teachers. Obedient little beggars! Rocky yelled at them again: "Get off the school ground, get out of sight!"

He turned back to look for more kids and was horrified to see blackened faces on some, and others with clothes still glowing. Several ran toward him with their hair in flames. He and the other teachers had no towels or blankets—they could only smother the flames with sleeves and bare hands. He kept the little bodies moving through the window frame—there was no time to check for minor, or even serious injuries. First priority was to get them out alive.

By this point, Rocky had only seen children who he knew had been on his side of the room. It was hard to feel any confidence that those closest to the fireball and the acrid smoke had survived. As it was, the smoke would overcome everyone if they didn't all get out soon.

In some ways, the children on the opposite side of the room had an advantage, because the doors allowed immediate escape, if only they could find them. Out in the hallway, Jack Mitchell was looking for his wife. "Have you seen Jean," he called to a figure running down the hall. He did not know she had been blasted toward the door, that Janel Dayton had tried and failed to help her, or that she had finally been able to half-crawl to safety by herself. The smoke-obscured figure passed him by without a response.

Running took on an almost mystical importance—if you could run, you could live. Kindergartner Johnny King ran into the schoolyard crying "I don't wanna die!" When he finally collapsed, it was at the feet of Judy Himmerich, his aunt.

"I don't know how I got out in the hallway," Kam Wixom said. "And I don't know why I turned north to those doors. I just found myself running." When he realized he was outside and safe, he yelled "I'm alive! I'm alive!" At the time, he thought he was running fast, but "I guess my legs were starting to go rubbery. I saw a little first grader tear past me toward Main Street. Being panic-stricken helped him run like I'd never seen him before."

Music teacher John Miller was trying to dismantle the rest of the barricade that Janel Dayton had been working on when she tried to help Jean Mitchell and was nearly overcome by smoke. John was desperate to pull the last chairs and tables apart so the exit was free.

At that moment, David Young's face appeared at the open restroom door. He was holding a .22 pistol in one hand and a .44 in the other. There was no recognition or reaction in his expression, but John knew, as he looked into David's face, that he was in trouble. Instantly, he turned and ran. At first, there was no place to go. He heard the gunshot and felt it "thud." Not certain he had actually been hit, he found his way outside and began to run. The smoke-free, clear spring air convinced him he was finally safe.

But this euphoria didn't last long. He began to feel more and more dizzy, even as he ran toward Main Street. Suddenly he collapsed, at the edge of Robinson's yard, almost at Janel Dayton's feet. Mrs. Dayton herself was still trying to catch her breath. Kam Wixom ran up just in time to see the EMTs sprint to Miller's aid. Finding blood from a bullet wound below his right shoulder blade, they loaded him in a waiting ambulance and rushed to Bear Lake Memorial Hospital, over the border in Montpelier, Idaho.

Watching near Kam was fellow-student Brenda Hartley. Kam was shocked and startled to see her blackened face, but she turned out not to be so much burned as smothered in soot. The plastic decoration on her T-shirt had melted in the heat.

Rocky Moore had finally pushed the last child he could see out the window. Still not sure just what to do, he decided to leave while he could. He took a deep breath and wriggled through the narrow opening, expecting to crash unceremoniously on the ground. Suddenly, he was caught. He felt a spurt of fear, imagining David Young approaching from behind, ready to wrestle him back into the room or shoot him as he tried to escape. Rocky looked back—there was no one—yet something was holding him fast.

Suddenly he recognized the loud crack of gunshots. Thinking it must be David, he battled with panic, trying to get out the window. But David wasn't there. What sounded like a spray of gunfire was in fact the hundreds of cartridges

Young had lined up against the classroom wall. In the soaring temperatures of the burning room, they were starting to explode spontaneously. Feeling along the window frame, Rocky realized he had only been stopped by his belt, which had caught on the protruding window latch. He freed it and tumbled to the grass in a heap. The minutes he was entangled had seemed like hours.

On the far side of the room, Eva Clark had been behind John Miller, when she realized Kathy was not at her side. She had no choice but to grope back into the stifling, acrid, half-blinding conflagration if she wanted to find her youngster alive. But in order to do so, she also had to pass Doris Young. Eva realized Doris must have taken the bomb's full force. She also knew there was nothing she could do for the woman who was suffering such agonizing pain. Her only duty now was to locate her four-year-old and escape. Poking around the room, she thought she saw a familiar form, then the little girl reached up. "Mamma!" she cried. Eva pulled her daughter free and pushed toward the exit where her other children were waiting.

There in the doorway was David, still holding a pistol in each hand. She knew she was completely defenseless—yet she thought she saw a look of surrender in his eyes that had not been there before. "I will never forget the man's face," she said, recalling the experience later. "It had the look of defeat. … His will to continue was shattered." She waited no longer, but turned her back on him, shielding the children, and hurried with them out the door. No gunshot followed their retreat. Soon, they were at the end of the hallway, and free.

On the lawn, Rocky Moore had picked himself up, and was glancing back through the window. He was amazed to see more youngsters arrive. This time he pulled them through from the outside, and as he did, saw someone who lifted his spirits greatly. It was Cindy Cowden, the young woman who was only in Cokeville that day because she wanted to teach elementary school. She had been on the far side of the room, and from her presence Rocky knew that at least some of those closest to the bomb had survived. Then he saw student teacher Kris Kasper come around the corner of the outside wall—another person who had been in a different part of the room from Rocky! He felt more hopeful that others, too, had survived.

Substitute teacher Pat Bennion was also at the windows, trying to lift children through. Badly hit by the fireflow down the wall when the bomb went off, she was too busy now, helping the children climb out, even to notice that her arms had been seared. The skin was becoming more and more abraded by repeated lifting and pushing across the window frame. She would need expert medical care, and soon.

One of the last to leave Room 4 was Verlene Bennion, the 66-year old teacher's aide. She suffered second degree burns on her arms and back, and had to be treated for smoke inhalation as well. She remembers feeling a great desire, as she worked her way toward the door, for every person in the room to live at least as long as she had up to that moment.

Once they were safely outside, some of the children living

in town ran directly home without even looking to see if their parents were among the crowd milling around the school. Conversely, many parents had left home and come to the police barricade, simply unable to wait passively for news.

Lowell Clark, alerted by his high school daughter, Beverly, was one of the crowd of some two hundred parents gathered outside the school grounds. He had no idea his wife Eva was inside the school with their children. Everyone nearby had heard the explosion. The sense of desperation and dread became more and more tangible as the seconds passed. Suddenly Lowell saw and heard bewildered children stream from the school and run towards them, sometimes to the first adult they could recognize, sometimes just to anyone who would wrap them in a safe embrace. Parents found it hard to recognize their own youngsters behind the blackened faces with burned clothes and singed hair that came stumbling up to them.

Lowell was amazed to see Eva leading their children from the school. How had she gotten there? But as he looked over his family with enormous relief and gratitude, his heart stopped. "Where's Christy?" he asked his wife. Eva had no idea. Both of them immediately began asking around in case someone had seen her. Eva was frightened she was back there in that room full of debris, and smoke, and possibly David Young. She couldn't bear to think she might have saved five of her children only to lose the sixth.

Returning teachers were no less agonized by fears that a child might have been left behind. As each of them safely escaped, he or she was besieged by anxious parents, all with the same question: "Where is my child???" Kliss Sparks could be heard above the general clamor shouting: "Fourth graders—over here!" Several students volunteered to look for the ones Mrs. Sparks couldn't find. Jack Mitchell was assembling his sixth graders, while Jean tried to take a mental count of her first graders. Some were still missing.

Several of the Main Street homes that bordered the schoolyard had been evacuated earlier when officials realized how powerful the deadman's bomb was. These homes were now turned into temporary treatment centers as the EMTs set up triage for the hostages. Those who did not need medical attention telephoned home, trying to find their parents. More often, their parents were already there, searching through the escaping children one by one, trying to be calm as the search sometimes stretched into hours. As the initial shock of the bomb blast and then the frantic escape wore off, students and teachers alike began to feel the extent of the injuries they had received.

From the moment the bomb exploded, EMTs, firemen and lawmen prepared and then attempted to get inside the building. Principal Excell had been on the telephone, talking to a newspaper reporter at the critical moment. "The bomb's exploded!" he yelled into the telephone, accidentally dropping it. Immediately he picked it up and called the town hall, repeating the identical message. Sheriff's Deputy Earl Carroll didn't need to be told. Those at the town hall heard the explosion clearly. It was impossible not to imagine the sounds of children screaming.

Excell grabbed his fire extinguisher and ran down the hall, but as soon as he saw the huge cloud of smoke bursting from Room 4, he gave up. Running outside, he saw law officers running toward him. Excell yelled at them to hurry. "I can hear ammo exploding," he said. "They must be shooting the children!"

While some of the officers were trying to get into Room 4, others were frantically trying to keep citizens from overrunning the building. Parents broke from the police cordon toward school entrances in a wall of anxiety. One father ran forward, cursing loudly. "I'm going in there after that SOB myself," he yelled. Police officers begged townspeople to stay back so that EMTs and firemen could get through.

Patrolman Brad Anderson knew he had to get in quickly. If David Young was there and still armed, he could be shooting randomly, just to take as many with him as possible. Anderson knew that half the problem would be the room itself—in the fiery and smoky aftermath, it would be just as easy to mistake a teacher or older student for Young as it would be to let David slip by, thinking he was one of them. Anderson wanted to prevent either of those things from happening.

He checked his bullet-proof vest and drew his service revolver. Sheriff's Deputy Greg Goodman joined him and the two stepped through the double doors into the school. Their first encounter was with a shadowy figure who fit the general description of David Young, but who turned out to be the father who had been threatening to search for his son. How he had gotten inside they couldn't be sure, but he was ordered out immediately and told he was lucky to be alive. His son, it turned out, was already on the way home—despite his ordeal, pedaling there on his own bike.

Patrolman Anderson didn't know that Police Chief Cal Fredrickson had returned and come directly to the school, still in his civilian clothes. He was already in the building, but coming from a different direction, moving toward the other two. Deputy Goodman, who lived in Kemmerer, didn't know Chief Fredrickson well, and the two men drew their pistols on each other as their paths converged. A second deadly accident was narrowly avoided, as Anderson identified the men to each other.

Anderson and Goodman were now able to move toward Room 4. Reaching it, Anderson opened the door while Goodman propped a chair against it. Brad had already decided that rushing into the center of the room would be wiser than peering around the corner of the door. The gunman would be seeing them against clear daylight. They would only be viewing an atmosphere the consistency of pea soup.

Just as they opened the door, both men heard a gunshot. Before either could react, layers of thick, oily smoke poured out. Anderson, unable to locate an air pack before going in, had never found breathing so difficult. The fumes were both piercing and unavoidable. He moved back, followed by

Goodman, and the two men pondered their next move. Then, from inside the room came a second shot. The door spring, which had begun pushing at the chair, forced it away completely. The door slammed shut.

Despite their need to get inside, both men decided to wait at least briefly for the smoke to clear. While they waited, someone at the far end of the hallway turned off the alarm bell. Earl Carroll had located the proper key. As they recovered their ability to breathe normally, Anderson and Goodman talked quietly, keeping a wary eye on both ends of the corridor. Suddenly a voice boomed down the hallway. "We've found one subject dead in the bathroom!" they heard.

Sheriff's Deputy Randy White had located an air pack, and gotten safe access to Room 4 just before Anderson and Goodman arrived. He could see no one moving about, so he approached the restroom door cautiously and pushed it open a crack. When this produced no response, he carefully peeked around the door. A man's body was slumped with its leg pressed against the doorway. This must be David Young.

Although certain David was dead, Randy took the precaution of placing his handcuffs around the man's wrists. He also removed the weapons in the bathroom including those on David's body. Beyond that he disturbed nothing, knowing the medical examiner would need the site intact.

Randy's next responsibility was to look for other bodies, a task he dreaded. "I had read many reports of children hiding in fear in out-of-the-way places following fires and explosions. Other lawmen and I now began searching all the little hiding places," he reported.

While Chief Fredrickson and Earl Carroll had not heard Randy White call out, and were thus searching the building in case David Young was holed up somewhere else, word was passed to Principal Excell outside that the building was secure. One critical phase of the day's work was over.

Firefighters and EMTs had also been trying to get to the schoolroom, knowing that there still might be people inside who could be saved if the fire and smoke were controlled. As the firemen hooked up their hoses, EMT Kevin Walker thought he heard two shots. Hoses were directed at the windows, but it was soon clear that too little water was getting into the room. Still not knowing whether it was safe to approach the windows, one of the EMTs moved to the larger section above and discovered it didn't open. Barely hesitating, he located a piece of metal pipe and broke the glass, wrestling out the steel frame with his bare hands. Now the firemen could get the water where it was needed.

As they manned the hoses, they thought they saw an adult woman's body on the floor near the far wall. At first it appeared she might be overcome with smoke inhalation. One of the EMTs thought she might still be saved with mouth-to-mouth resuscitation. "But we soon realized the futility," Kevin Walker said. "Air being breathed in was escaping through a hole in her head." The whole top of her skull was missing.

Fireman Allen Burton feared it was his sister, kindergarten teacher Kim Kasper. To make identification easier, the woman's body was pulled through the window and carried on a blanket to the lawn. Adult hostages were asked to look at the body to help make identification certain. All agreed. "That's the woman holding us hostage," they told investigators. Though badly burned, her face was still recognizable.

While the crucial identifications of David and Doris Young were being made, allowing lawmen to verify that the crisis was officially over, Lowell and Eva Clark were still searching frantically for Christy. They had split up in order to cover more territory, and were now wondering if police would let them into the school to search for her personally. Before trying to get that permission, however, Eva was approached by a friend who had been entrusted with a message for her—Lowell had found their daughter alive. She was burned—he didn't know how badly—and was being taken by ambulance to Star Valley Hospital in Afton, Wyoming, 50 miles away. Lowell had located her just in time to ride along. Greatly relieved, Eva quickly arranged to leave for Afton herself.

While the hostages had by far the more serious injuries—Deputy Ron Hartley, for instance, learned that all four of his grade school children had been taken to Bear Lake Memorial Hospital in Montpelier—those assigned to search and restore order also suffered from the experience. One of the lawmen was hospitalized for smoke inhalation; Patrolman Anderson was treated for nearly an hour on the grounds of the school for the same problem. As the crisis phase passed and the search and recovery phase moved forward, parents continued to look for missing children, slowly sorting out who had been taken to which hospital and why.

Two of the most badly burned, Billie Jo Hutchinson and Tina Morfeld, were rushed to expert care immediately. In time, 79 of the hostages were hospitalized and the most critical were transferred to the University of Utah Burn Center in Salt Lake City.

Normal human error occasionally crept in, making already tense and hurting people dig even deeper for patience and stamina. Colleen King, already at the hospital in Montpelier visiting her sick father, was told to stand by: her sons had been burned from a bomb explosion at their school in Cokeville, and were on their way to the hospital. Only after waiting an hour and half for them to arrive did Colleen learn that Montpelier was the wrong destination—they had been taken to the hospital in Kemmerer.

While the hostages were being identified and treated, as swiftly and carefully as their situations permitted, everyone still had their minds on what the lawmen and investigators were finding in Room 4. The only question of any importance continued to be: who was still inside?

As lawmen, firemen, and EMTs picked through the room rubble, their minds were on the same question. The first impression was that of total shambles. While the walls were still upright, much of the ceiling tile had blown out. Debris was everywhere, and everything was black, except for one white patch on the east wall about the size of a human figure with its arms partially outstretched. In the smoke-stained wreckage, this area stood out sharply. It was speculated that the blast had spent its force on some person, most likely Doris Young, leaving the wall area behind that person unseared. But Doris had been in the center of the room. The mystery remained unsolved.

As they worked, searchers continued to be amazed at the destruction in the room. Obviously, property damage was almost total (the estimate was later placed at $50,000). With so much destroyed, how had anyone escaped alive, let alone the number of people who did? Patrolman Anderson kept his mind focused on the task, moving slowly and methodically through everything on the floor. Yet every back pack or abandoned jacket made his heart jump—was he coming now to the body of a child?

Finally, the lawmen and their co-searchers turned over the last bit of flotsam, examined next to and under the last bit of broken furniture large enough to shield a body, and investigated the far reaches of the last closet. Only then did they dare believe the unbelievable: there were no bodies in the room. Every one of the hostages had gotten out alive.

The good news raced through town, turning what had been dreadful hours of pressure and uncertainty into relief, gratitude and tears, all to be shared with neighbors and friends, more than likely in the same position themselves. The official investigation was barely under way, but lawmen could now turn to the work ahead with confidence in their professionalism, without the fury and pain they expected to feel as soon as they heard the bomb explode.

Their first task was getting rid of the left-over ammunition. The cartridges had already spent themselves by exploding in the heat of the fire inside Room 4. Some of the blasting caps, however, had not detonated, and these were quickly taken care of, in specially-designed bomb-disposal canisters, in a nearby field. David's arsenal of rifles and other guns, no longer a threat to anyone, was taken into evidence.

Whatever remained of the bomb was the next object of investigation. Explosives expert Richard Haskell from Rock Springs, Wyoming was put in charge. A member of the Sweetwater County Sheriff's Office, he had become familiar with bomb design during military service and during his years as a lawman. The deadman's bomb used by David Young was a most familiar type.

As he dismantled the remains of the device, however, Richard found something strange. The two wires which were to detonate two blasting caps, and fill the air with exploding gunpowder, were severed, cut cleanly, as if snipped with wire cutters. When the battery current could not reach these two caps, there was no power to spray their contents into the room, or the aluminum dust either, which was supposed to increase the incendiary potential of the air when the bomb went off.

Had the blast occurred as David originally designed it, Haskell said, it "would have caused an explosion caving in the walls and blowing up everything in the room." Further, Haskell found that leakage in the plastic jug used by David to contain the gasoline component of the bomb had created a partial paste of the granules which were supposed to become airborne at detonation. The bomb had been designed to kill everyone in the room, Haskell concluded, but in those two ways alone it had been prevented from working as David intended.

In time, official investigations would reveal more unusual aspects to the entire incident, but at the moment it was the children who began to make statements their parents found remarkable, to say the least.

Seven-year-old Katie Walker told her fourteen-year-old brother, Shane, the first family member she saw after running from the explosion, "They saved us. I said a prayer, and they saved us!"

"Who saved you?" Shane asked.

"The angels," she replied.

Katie saw her mother, Glenna Walker, the recently-certified EMT, a few minutes later. "Mommy," Katie repeated, "the angels saved us!"

Glenna patted her daughter on the head. "Yes, we all have much to be grateful for, dear," she said, holding her close.

Glenna did not realize that her daughter wanted to be taken literally. Even though Katie's sister Rachel was being treated for burns at the hospital, Rachel and Katie and Travis had all come through their ordeal alive and Glenna hoped they would soon no longer need to talk about the takeover. The children, however, wanted to talk about it.

Dr. Vern Cox was one of the psychologists brought in to help the town work through the fears and feelings generated by David Young's attack. Along with other families in Cokeville, Kevin and Glenna joined the group and individual discussions intended to provide this help. At one of these meetings, Katie and Rachel told Dr. Cox that they had tried to talk with their parents about the angels who had saved them. Their brother Travis also had something very serious on his mind. Dr. Cox told their parents what the children had been telling him.

"Why haven't they been telling us, their own parents?" Glenna wanted to know.

"Have you been listening to them?" he asked her. "Really listening?"

Glenna realized that perhaps they hadn't. She and Kevin arranged a time when the whole family could talk.

"They were standing there above us," Katie began. "There was a mother and a father and a lady holding a tiny baby, and a little girl with long hair. There was a family of people. The woman told us the bomb was going off soon, and to listen to our brother. He was going to come over and tell us what to do."

"She said to be sure we did what he told us," Rachel added.

"They were all dressed in white, bright like a light bulb but brighter around the face," Katie told her mother.

"The girl had a long dress," Rachel nodded, "which covered her feet, and she had light brown hair." The two girls spoke quietly but firmly about people who had certainly not been among the hostage group in Room 4. There was no apology or self-consciousness—the people they described seemed as real to them as their own parents, who were listening, attentively now. Rachel remembered something else—that the figures dressed in white standing above them had moved around to another part of the room just before the bomb went off.

Some time later, the authors of this book met with the Walkers to ask them about their roles as EMTs during the hostage crisis. At that visit, their children's unique comments were mentioned. Permission was asked to discuss their experiences with them. Glenna and Kevin were understandably reluctant to subject their children to the scrutiny of others about something personal and sacred, even if those people knew and cared about them. But Katie had a different idea. "The woman made me feel good. I knew she loved me. I want to talk about it." Rachel and Travis agreed.

Accordingly, on December 28, 1986 we went to the Walkers, taking our son Kamron and daughter Cindy with us. After the children played together for awhile, we asked Travis what he had seen, and whether he could describe it to us. "I didn't see anything—nothing!" he emphasized. "I just heard a voice. It told me to find my little sisters and take them over by the window and keep them there. I did what I was told. I looked around and found them and told them to follow me over by the window."

He seemed absorbed. I had known Travis for five years

and had never seen him look that serious before. "I told them to stay there and not move," he said.

"Did they respond?" we asked.

"They were playing with their friends, and I didn't think they would want to leave them. I knew they had to come with me. They got their coloring pages and I took them over by the windows."

"Did they stay right there?" my wife asked.

Both girls quickly said "Yes."

"But," Travis continued, "I didn't stay there with them. I was also told to help them through the window when the bomb went off. And I went back over with the other boys where I had been, by the door...."

Glenna interrupted. "That was when he told Dr. Cox how terribly guilty he felt—that he had not been by the windows with his sisters when the bomb exploded." There was a long silence.

"I should have gone over by the window with my sisters. That's what I was told to do. I didn't do it." Glenna told us there was no consolation for Travis in the weeks following the hostage crisis. He did not sleep well for awhile, she said. "I have never seen him so upset."

The girls seemed content to discuss their experience at length. They remembered details vividly. Referring to the people they had seen, they were asked "How did they come into the room? Was it through the main door or the door by the bathroom?"

"Through the ceiling," both girls said at once.

"Where were they standing?"

Katie held her hand about two feet off the ground, just below her waist. "They were about this high off the ground."

"Could you see all of them, their entire bodies?"

Rachel nodded, then said as though deep in thought, "Except for the little girl. She had a long white dress. I couldn't see her feet."

"Was there any color at all in the clothing they wore?"

Rachel shook her head. "They were all dressed in white."

Kevin suggested looking at some old photos of family members, both living and deceased. Katie did not require a lengthy look as she picked up an old picture in a locket. She didn't talk for a moment, but studied it as if enjoying a happy memory. Then, "She looked like this, only she didn't wear glasses." Rachel, who had been out of the room briefly, came back in and looked at the photo herself. "That's the angel! But without the glasses," she said emphatically.

Shirley Ruth Thornock, the woman in the picture, was Glenna's mother, who had died when Glenna was only sixteen. "My mother never lived to know my family," Glenna said.

Another photo, this one of Kevin's brother who died in 1961, "looked like" the man who was with the "family of angels," the girls said. But they hadn't looked at him that day as closely as the woman who was doing the talking. They couldn't be sure. There was no explanation for the others mentioned in the group. The girls had never seen nor known any of the others they described, including the little girl with the long brown hair.

I had to ask the traditional question: "Did they have wings?"

"No!" the two girls said without hesitation. "They looked like we do, but all dressed in white," Rachel said.

"Did she smile at you," I asked, referring to the "angel mother."

Katie pondered the question. "She sort of smiled at me with her voice."

"Did she make you feel you were going to be safe?"

"She said we would be," Rachel replied, "if we did what our brother told us."

We turned to Travis. "Travis, did you feel that you would be protected when the bomb went off?"

"I knew, somehow, we would be if I followed directions. When I heard the explosion, I just forgot about part of what I was supposed to do. I was so close to the hallway, it was easy to get out there...it was a minute later when I thought about my sisters."

"Were all the angels there when the bomb went off?" Kevin Walker asked his daughters.

"I don't know," Rachel replied. "The smoke from the bomb covered them up."

It was getting close to the little girls' bedtime. We had talked together for more than an hour, on a subject both sensitive and unusual.

The Walkers expressed their own feelings about what their children had reported. Said Glenna, "The children know it happened, and they want to share it. They feel they have a responsibility to share it so others can benefit from it. What others do with their experiences or feelings is up to them."

Kevin pointed out: "It was the children's decision. They stand behind it. We stand behind them. Where would we be—where would any of us be—without the courage to testify of such a spiritual happening?"

Other children than the Walker threesome spoke of "messengers" who appeared to them as well. Some families decided it was too personal a matter to put on record. One mother said some people would not comprehend what the children were saying or know what to do with the information. Several other parents said their children gave specific details of someone they didn't know appearing to them in the hostage room. These families specifically requested that their names not be used.

One child who was willing to share his spiritual experience in surviving the takeover was six-year-old Nathan Hartley. Nathan was sitting near the taped line before the bomb detonated. He told his father, veteran sheriff's investigator Ron Hartley, what he saw.

"The lady helped me get out alive," he reported.

"I've been through it all with hours of interrogating suspects and prisoners," Hartley said. "I'm especially trained to detect lying or manipulative answers for personal gain. I asked some more questions."

The first grader continued: "A lady told me the bomb was

going to go off very soon. She told me how to save myself. She said to go over by the window, then hurry out when I heard the bomb explode. She told me that I would make it if I did exactly what she said." Nathan said he had never seen the woman before. As the Walkers had, Ron Hartley leafed through the family album with his son. At one page, Nathan stopped his father. "That's her," he explained abruptly. It was a picture of Flossie Elliott, Nathan's great-grandmother. She had been dead for three years.

In January 1987, Nathan drew a picture of the way it had been. It shows a bright angel over the head of Doris. The stick figures in front represent the students—he didn't see an angel over David's head. Did the Hartleys feel any concern about relating their son's unique experience? "It happened," Mrs. Hartley said. "I'd rather face people now than explain, either here or in the next life, why we didn't say something about it," Hartley emphasized. "We can't back down from personal convictions."

Three weeks after the takeover, Nathan wrote down specifics of his experience. "Just before the bombs went off," he wrote, "angels came down through the ceiling. They were bright like light bulbs. There were about ten of them holding hands around the children to protect them." One of the angels "told me the bomb was going to go off.... All the angels told us to run to the windows when the bomb went off. I was just getting ready to run to the window when it went off."

Later, he wrote, "What I saw was that there were robe-clad

1 Nathan's Angel
2 Door to Hall
3 Bomb
4 Cart
5 Taped Square
6 Hostage Children
7 Escape Window
8 Restroom Door
9 Doris Young with bomb attached to wrist

people by almost everyone. I looked around and saw that some were floating in air. I suddenly realized that these people were angels. I looked toward the taped square and saw an angel high above Doris Young. It seemed as if the angel were about to leave."

Years later, when asked about the unique vision, he described it as a "special and sacred experience. ... For those who want to be benefited by it, that is what happened."

Eva Clark was intrigued with the sensations she had felt while a prisoner of David Young. "I was scared," she said with no reservations. "I was really scared. He had made sure we adults understood that he would not hesitate to shoot us. I was sure we were going to die. For about an hour and a half, time seemed to drag by, if not stand still altogether. But the last hour or so, after praying over and over, [I felt] entirely different. I felt peace. I knew we would make it."

Eva also spoke feelingly of the statements made by the children. "Everyone involved in the investigation of David Young's bomb knows something strange and unexplainable happened. No one has any plausible idea at all how the children safely escaped. I think it is time to listen to them, the hostage children themselves, and let them tell us the reason they all survived. We can label it 'divine intervention' or whatever we want. Whatever we call it, many of these explanations from the children help everything fit together better."

Two other adults found themselves greatly affected by their hostage experience, Rocky Moore and Jack Mitchell. Moore had long joked that he would believe in a God only when he saw his personal "burning bush." He had used the expression every time he needed to avoid a discussion of spiritual things. Now, he wanted to talk about spiritual things. At a high school football game which took place several months after the crisis, someone asked Rocky "What was it that saved you from the bomb?"

"I'll tell you what happened," he told his questioner. "God was looking out for his kids."

"And you were saved because you were with them?" a bystander wanted to know.

"Exactly," Rocky replied.

"Did you see your burning bush, Rocky?" a child who had been one of the hostages asked.

"You bet I did!" the teacher nearly shouted. "That's enough for me or anybody. And don't you forget it!"

After falling from the classroom escape window, Rocky carried his sprained arm around in a sling. Once mended, he seemed as feisty as ever, but almost contentedly ecstatic with memories of the experience. "I don't see," he said at one point, "how there could be any more atheists left in this country."

His former fellow-agnostic, Jack Mitchell, made his change of heart unmistakably clear. In a statement repeated in three different interviews made over several weeks' time, he stated, "I know this; there is no other explanation for what happened. It was divine intervention. A higher power stepped in. We could do nothing for ourselves. There were prayers answered in there. I'll never doubt the power of prayer again."

It would perhaps be easy to discount the hostage children's accounts because of their age, or their willingness to please, or their need to make sense of a terrible ordeal by investing it with some eternal significance. It would be equally easy to discount their parents' support because parents are not sufficiently objective to properly judge, or because it's not always possible to determine whether your children are a bit confused, or innocently play-acting, or actually telling non-collusive lies. And it might be easy to discount sheriff's investigator Hartley's professional approach to his son's reported experience, because, just by being the boy's father, his detachment might be questioned.

But the evidence of bomb expert Richard Haskell would also have to be discounted. And he concluded that the explanation for the discrepancy between the effect of the bomb, had it gone off as David designed it, and the effect the bomb actually had, is not to be found in science. His investigations pointed out fourteen factors which unexpectedly minimized the impact of the blast on the hostages, the first of which is the unexplained fact that the blasting-cap connecting wires were cut straight through, when there was no opportunity for that to have happened during the siege. (See Appendix II for a complete list of the fourteen factors.)

Haskell issued this statement: "I don't know how the wires were cut. My only official conclusion is that I can't begin to explain it." At one time he said to television reporters, "The whole thing just appears to be a miracle." Asked later about his use of the word, Haskell not only stood by his statement, but underscored it. "To be more specific," he said, "labeling it a miracle is the understatement of the century."

Chapter Five

"LOVE POURS IN"

"Our freedom was intact, our children were alive. Pain would pass, burns would heal. God does hear and answer prayers."
—*Sherrie Cornia, mother of three hostages*

The townspeople of Cokeville had every reason to feel jubilant. By attacking its children, David Young had attacked the whole community and placed its very existence in jeopardy. Even though the siege had lasted less than three hours, every hostage was in grave jeopardy while it lasted. Five minutes of genuine danger can be frightening enough. Three hours must have seemed, to the captives inside, helpless to break free, and their families outside, helpless to aid them, an eternity of fear and frustration.

Had most or all of the hostages died, it is not impossible to imagine the town dying with them. It would be too painful to stay in a place that only reminded survivors of how much they had lost. Townsfolk exulted, therefore, when they fully understood how marvelous the escape from the school had been: 150-odd children and adults, trapped in a single room as a bomb designed for maximum destruction went off inside it. By surviving their ordeal, the victims of David Young had turned their town into a symbol of something extraordinarily powerful: not the explosive force of the bomb itself, but the transcending force of the love which unified the hostages and gave them the courage and wit to outlast their attackers.

Sharing the wonder and jubilation felt by the community, people from surrounding towns and from all over the world poured out their feelings in letters, greeting cards, posters, banners, phone calls and personal visits. The support shown the hostages came in a flood of incredible intensity. Extended family members kept Cokeville's phone lines hot with messages of hope and concern. Encouragement came from old friends, stunned by news which struck so close to home. People from all over felt compassion and empathy, and took the time to express it.

One letter included a warm and sensitive poem about courage and a reminder that "what we make of ourselves with the time given in this life is what matters most." The letter was permeated with love. It was written by a youngster dying of leukemia.

Numerous letters included money, donated to help alleviate the mounting medical costs of those injured in the flames. A fund was set up for "The Cokeville Kids." From coast to coast, messages and donations swamped the little post office—over $16,000 was collected in the first few days. The money that flowed in was enough to cover hospital and doctor expenses for every child injured. These gifts from well-wishing strangers were especially appreciated, because some of the most serious injuries involved children from families who were out of work or struggling.

A Lutheran minister sent heartfelt wishes from his congregation: "We will be praying for all of you in church Sunday. God bless, as you now attempt to recover and to put yesterday in the past. Have a good day and a better tomorrow."

And the pastor of St. Margaret Mary Church in Algonquin, Illinois shared a poignant message from his parishioners: "Our parish community has witnessed the power of prayer...part of our parish were members of the pilgrimage group hijacked on TWA's flight 847 last June. Therefore, we are very understanding of what you have just gone through."

Some months after the bombing, a fifteen-foot-long banner arrived from a Latter-day Saint primary in Bakersfield, California. Covered with hearts, and the words "Our hearts reach out to you...," it bore photos of dozens of children aged three to twelve. Messages with the photos indeed warmed the hearts of their readers: "I'm nine years old. I am glad you are safe." From other nine-year-olds: "...glad you are all rite," and "My name is Mike. I am glad you guys didn't die." An eleven-year-old drew a hand-held bomb: "I hope you are OK. You are lucky the bomb didn't work. P.S. Come to Bakersfield. You'll like it." Another invitation was even more compelling: "Please come to Bakersfield and see my skateboard." Teachers of the organization wrote "Our primary loves you all! Best wishes to you!!"

A man in California, who preferred to remain anonymous, sent each of the worst burn victims a cabbage patch doll, not purchased from the store, but donated from his own private, highly treasured collection—twelve in all. He said he wanted to help the Cokeville kids cope. Such expressions as these without doubt helped the victims heal. They saw tangible evidence pour in which proved that, even if there were demented strangers out there who might bring them harm, there were also many, many more caring, genuinely concerned and loving strangers who would sacrifice personal time and means to bring them joy. This outpouring of love set the town on the first steps to recovery.

Before the hostages and their families could put the anger of the takeover behind them, however, they would have to go through a period of difficult coping. Everyone was pretty much in agreement by now that something extremely unusual, something which had all the characteristics of genuine divine intervention, had taken place. That protection had accomplished its task and was now, perhaps, withdrawn. Responsibility for coming all the way out from under the shadow of David Young was now in the hands of the victims and townsfolk themselves.

Effects of the ordeal didn't take long to manifest themselves. Psychologists familiar with hostage trauma know that, as bad as physical injuries can be, the accompanying emotional injuries can be much more destructive and long-lasting. While similar in many respects, there would also be some important differences between the emotional trauma which the victims suffered and the trauma their friends and families went through, waiting for the crisis to end.

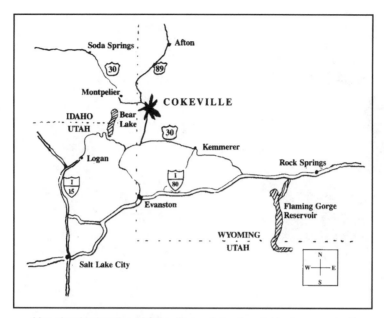

Map showing location of Cokeville in relation to neighboring communities.

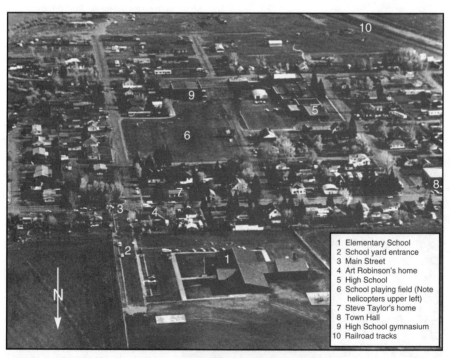

1 Elementary School
2 School yard entrance
3 Main Street
4 Art Robinson's home
5 High School
6 School playing field (Note
   helicopters upper left)
7 Steve Taylor's home
8 Town Hall
9 High School gymnasium
10 Railroad tracks

Aerial view of Cokeville Main Street. Library, post office, and stores are to the west (right) along the street. (East across U.S. Highway 30 is Smith's Fork Road, Pine Creek, and the town cemetery on the bluff of Big Hill.) (Gerald Silver photo courtesy of Deseret News.)

David Young, a police file photo.

Although his wrist was attached to the trigger of a lethal bomb, David Young chose to further impress hostages with these weapons leaning against the wall of the first grade classroom. (Dan Dockstader photo courtesy of Star Valley Independent.)

(Left) Gina Taylor manages a courageous smile from her hospital bed, although bandages swath burned face and hands. Doctors wondered if she would lose sight in her right eye—she didn't. (JM Heslop photo courtesy Deseret News)

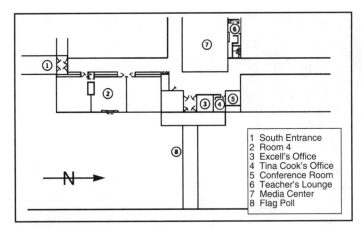

(Left) Floor plan of Cokeville Elementary School shows south wing of classroom including besieged Room 4 and Mrs. Cook's receptionist desk.

1 South Entrance
2 Room 4
3 Excell's Office
4 Tina Cook's Office
5 Conference Room
6 Teacher's Lounge
7 Media Center
8 Flag Poll

(Right) Room 4
Classroom designed for 35 students became a frightening prison for 154 hostages. With arms and legs overlapping, the hostages waited out the diabolical plot of David Young, seven years in the planning.
Each X represents a hostage. David Young is shown in the large square. (Drawn to scale.)

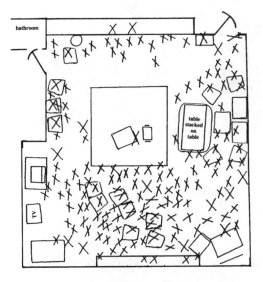

Child's-eye view of the bomb which threatened their lives.
(Drawing by Kamron Wixom)

(Left) Meaghen Thompson is one of Jean's best huggers, but fear and distrust have become part of some of the children's lives since David Young tried to force his "superior intellect" on unwilling hostages. Love strong enough to overcome those fears will be Jean's top priority now. (Ravell Call photo courtesy of Deseret News)

(Above) Rubble is all that remains of the once-threatening bomb cart. The device's design was intended to destroy the entire south wing of the school. (Dan Dockstader photo, Star Valley Independent.)

Although Jeremiah Moore's seventh birthday was not too happy, future birthdays are bound to be better. (Jack Monson photo courtesy Deseret News)

Town Hall is the scene of a press conference conducted by Lincoln County Sheriff T. Deb Wolfley. The room is filled with television and newspaper reporters, lawmen and investigators...

...and the arsenal collected from school and Young's van. In addition to rifles and numerous handguns, cans of gun powder and other bomb components, lawmen also collected three volumes on bomb construction and over a dozen diaries kept by the terrorists. (Ravell Call photos courtesy of Deseret News)

The American and Wyoming State flags fly briskly in the spring breeze while the body of Doris Young lies covered (white blanket) in the schoolyard. Meanwhile, lawmen discuss next move.

(Left) Sheriff Deb Wolfley explains findings of investigations to press (Dan Dockstader photo courtesy Star Valley Independent)

(Right) Billie Jo Hutchinson's face says it all. In spite of the Jobst bandage that would cover her more than a year, her smile and bright eyes promise a better tomorrow. (Jack Monson photo courtesy Deseret News)

Media from across the nation question investigators on the bomb used to threaten Cokeville hostages. (Tom Smart photo courtesy Deseret News)

Scenes from the movie
To Save the Children.

David Young (Richard
Thomas) shows Jake
Downey (Robert Urich)
the trigger mechanism
to his bomb. "We're
only one-half inch from
death."

David Young, anxious
for others to recognize
his superior intellect,
gleefully expounds his
philosophies of life
and death.

Jake races after a boy
who has returned to the
bombed-out room in
search of his missing
sister.

Pistol in hand, possibly for emphasis, Young reads his "zero equals infinity" philosophy.

Pushing the "dead man's" bomb in front of him and with Jake and others already as hostages, Young declares, "This is a revolution."

(Left) Jake stumbles through the haze of smoke in the confusion of the aftermath.

(Right) Jake's wife rushes to greet him as he realizes it's finally over.

The most common problem faced by hostage victims is an overwhelming sense of fear and vulnerability. Tina Cook, first to be confronted by David Young and first to be taken hostage, found returning to her school duties difficult. One day a man stepped up to the receptionist's desk and seemed to her to be stalling. She panicked. Finally, he asked for Mr. Excell—he was just there to check out the playground equipment.

On another day, while Tina was speaking with a visitor, the woman fished around in her purse. Tina immediately imagined a gun. When the woman found what she wanted, it was a business card: she was a sales representative on call. In addition to incidents like these, Tina had recurring nightmares of David Young walking up and thumping on the counter. "Here I am, Mrs. Cook," he would say, "and you didn't think I'd come back, did you?" It took her months to get the man's arrogant superiority and the fear she felt that day out of her mind.

One of the custodians for the school, whose child had been a hostage, told Principal Excell she could not work in the building any more after dark. The principal himself said it gave him "an eerie feeling" to turn a key in the school door when he came there alone several days after the takeover "with the memories so fresh in my mind."

Memorial Day, ten days after the incident, resulted in nervous moments for some of the hostage boys, but at the same time allowed them to move past their fears. The local Boy Scouts were asked to assist the American Legion post in commemorating the community dead. The boys felt very lucky not to be among those honored that year. At the appropriate moment in the ceremonies came a 21-gun salute. It sounded "a little too close" to the young assistants. "I jumped when the guns blew off near me," one boy said. "But we made it. I think we're going to be OK."

One kindergartner would have a much harder time recovering. Her personality changed after the takeover—not even her own family members could find the old enthusiasm in her. "The burns had healed. The rest hadn't," her mother said. Outgoing no longer, the little girl shut herself into a shell, hiding anytime she saw a man with a beard. When her father talked to a bearded man at their front door one day, she ran for a back bedroom. Hearing a firecracker at a family party, she disappeared and couldn't be found. After a long search, family members found her cowering in the barn.

Townspeople were counseled that every person would move at his own pace, and that traumatic events had anniversaries: "A year from now, for example, people will probably show increased anxiety."

Along with fear and anxiety, anger is recognized as an equally prevalent and genuine response to being victimized. At a town meeting held the Monday after the takeover, one citizen who had not been a hostage tried to apply some Christian charity by saying that perhaps the hostage-takers "didn't really want to hurt you."

The response was immediate, almost harsh: "How can anyone say they didn't mean to hurt us? They hauled all that crap in to kill people...!"

A five-year-old watched his father carry the body of a woman from the smoking classroom, taking "good care" of her. Then the boy realized the woman was the one who had tried to kill them. What did that say about his father? Another child named his emotion: he was "awfully, awfully mad."

In addition, there were the memories of terror and revulsion. Some children had crawled across a body and had attempted to help her, only to discover it was the woman who had threatened them. Such memories are not easily forgotten.

Problems would show up for months, even years—lives of the hostage families were not yet their own. Fathers and mothers, in search of security, found themselves putting down tougher rules. Mothers would jump at the falling of a pencil; fathers berate them for being so touchy. Mothers got after fathers for being insensitive. Even weeks after the crisis, a mother said she cried at nothing. Confessed another, "I snap at every little thing." Such behavior, even when recognized, left the victims feeling guilty, further lowering their self-esteem.

Emotional trauma was especially hard to overcome when it involved a loss of trust. Teachers who had been taken captive struggled with this as much as the children did. Janel Dayton reported that yearbook photographers had nearly given her a heart attack by taking an impromptu flash picture of her working in her room. One day the grandmother of one of her students arrived unannounced to fetch her grandchild. "I'd never seen her before," Mrs. Dayton said. "She could have done that in the past and it wouldn't have mattered, but things were different now."

The younger children had special problems to overcome. Those aged six and seven were just beginning to build a sense of confidence and order in their lives. Now both were, if not shattered, at least shaken. Trust, in particular, was damaged. Love and obedience were now suspect. "We did what the adults told us to do, and we got hurt," was expressed by some. "What did we do wrong?" Many of the children began to feel guilty; they were taken hostage because, in some unknown way, they hadn't "measured up."

Children who had been some of Jean Mitchell's best huggers began to hold back. They were now aloof, sharing less love. She sorely missed their expressions of simple love. Yet she knew those emotions couldn't be forced. Jean felt the kids might be feeling betrayed by the world of grownups that had let this thing happen to them. She was fearful about the youngsters losing trust in her. They had obeyed her, with this result. She was not sure what she could say to them.

The slow process of working through fears and hostilities generated by the crisis went on among those who had not been taken hostage as well. Fear that manifested itself among the victims as a frightening sense of vulnerability often manifested itself as overprotectiveness in the parents. Time and time again, mothers and fathers faced the mental hurdle of never wanting to let their young children out of sight, of not wanting to let them go back to school. Something as simple and familiar as a sonic boom could raise waves of panic and an intense desire to drop everything else and run to the child.

The anger felt by victims mirrored the anger felt by their families. One did not have to be present in the classroom to feel the trauma there, counselors explained. "Families and people who were outside of the town when things were happening will still have some very real and important feelings that need to be worked through."

Sam Bennion had reason to be angry. His wife Pat was substituting for Briant Teichert, away at the track meet, when the takeover occurred. She had to be hospitalized, and suffered complications from the infections in her arms. His widowed mother, Verlene, was in school as teacher's aide, and was injured while helping children escape through the windows. All three of the Bennion kids were among the hostages. Realistically, Sam had been threatened with the loss of his entire family. The anger and fear generated by that threat would not easily pass.

Delayed complications were often exhibited by parents rather than hostages. A number of adults were traumatized almost as much by what their mature imaginations told them could have happened, as they were by what actually did. Thinking about the awful possibilities became a coping mechanism of its own, as the mind tried to admit the existence of unthinkable scenarios in order to face them down.

Understandably, some who entirely escaped the crisis had to struggle with feeling left out—unworthy of the test. The six children absent that day had missed the most important, dramatic thing ever to happen to their community. Morning kindergartners, eluding capture by half a day, felt the same— no one was paying attention to them. Had they also "not measured up" somehow?

The name given to reactions like these, which seem so inconsistent on the surface, is "survivor guilt." Most often seen in those who live when their fellow-hostages die in a violent confrontation, survivor guilt also hits those who are simply not involved while their friends or loved ones are suffering. No one in Cokeville envied those who had been burned in the aftermath of the explosion. Yet they wanted to know first hand what had happened; they wanted to share the burden. Briant Teichert's absence from school the day of the takeover was particularly hard on him. The thought, he said, of substitute teacher Pat Bennion being harmed while taking his place "was just unbearable."

Older students, who felt guilty about not helping rescue their younger brothers and sisters, were themselves helped toward a more balanced frame of mind by the attending psychologists and counselors. "What if you had gone back," they were asked, "into the burning room?" "Wouldn't you just be in the way of people trying to get out quickly?" As the students answered such questions, they were able to realize that it was, indeed, unselfish to care so much about the other pupils, but that they did the right thing in getting quickly out of the way.

Families had to deal with the mundane responsibilities of daily life while they were also dealing with the serious emotional and physical burdens which the crisis forced upon them. One father, whose daughter was being treated for burns, later had a car wreck and had to be hospitalized himself—about the same time that his wife went to the hospital to give birth to unexpected twins. Fortunately for everyone, the showering of outside love and aid meant that no family had to lose their home or go hungry because they happened to cross the path of a confused and self-destructive man.

Occasionally, denial was seen as a practical way out of the crisis: "Let's not make too much of this whole thing. The kids are lucky to be alive. Let's forget about it and get on with our lives. The sooner we do it, the sooner the kids can do it." While the attitude was healthy in its effort not to wallow or dwell on the traumatic memories of their captive hours, most hostages and their parents realized that negative emotions were rising to the surface naturally and continually, and that it would be necessary to work through them, rather than deny them, before real healing could occur.

But the process could begin immediately. From the moment the children escaped and commenced the process of confronting what they had just experienced, parents and school officials in the town and psychologists who came from outside began a process of their own—offering the hostages positive ways of handling their physical and emotional upheaval.

Early on, townspeople were commended for immediately providing two positive experiences for the hostages. The first was total reassurance and the second was proper praise. When parents and other citizens were on hand to scoop up the first screaming youngster that crossed their paths, cuddling them personally and/or staying close while their parents were located, they provided crucial contrast to the detached, depersonalized malevolence David Young had shown. Familiar faces, familiar surroundings, behavior the children recognized as consistent and normal, even the sounds and smells they were used to, helped them accept that they had really escaped from Room 4. However frequently they would relive the fear of their hours with David Young, they would also be able to relive the memory of people who welcomed them unconditionally back to normal life.

Lincoln County Attorney Richard Leonard noted with amazement how well the local people were coping, even just after the takeover. "Here were people, in terror of their lives just two hours before," he said, "now serving drinks and sandwiches to out-of-town officials. They were bouncing back awfully fast, considering the circumstances. It was gratifying to see them recovering so quickly."

At the town meeting held the Monday after the crisis, everyone gathered to more formally assess what had happened. Dr. Allen Lowe, the District School Superintendent, assured the listeners that "you have the prayers and support of many. There were many heroes to come out of the tragedy last Friday, including you and your children. Our purpose is to rebuild, restore, and strengthen."

At one point, teachers were singled out for their heroic efforts, particularly those which kept themselves and the children calm in the face of danger. The audience rose to applaud them. The children themselves were praised for obeying teachers and summoning up a brave front for each other. Peace officers from other areas, who had come in to assist Cokeville's lawmen, praised the entire town for its discipline. "You were a great example," one of them said.

Someone stood to commend the EMTs for their work, then another spoke in praise of the law enforcement people. Everyone was thanking everyone. "In the eyes of professionals around the country who have handled very serious situations, you are to be commended," said Dr. Nohl Sandahl, head of the team of psychologists. "They stand in respect for how you have come out of this situation. You did things right." Teachers wanted to convince the children that they had experienced a severe trial and passed it with flying colors. Parents and other adults were counseled to show confidence: children can handle what parents can handle, townspeople were reminded.

Talking and listening, as the townspeople did at this meeting, was the next critical step in healing. Shock was wearing off. People needed to tell each other where they were when the bomb went off. Never had so much happened in such a short time in the town. Never had so many intense and diverse emotions been generated.

Rocky Moore took what he called a "realistic" attitude. "I wish David Young was here right now. Take away his guns and I'd like to have my hands on him—right now."

"Do you hate him?" Rocky was asked.

"You bet I do. I love hating him." At least Rocky could talk in a positive way about the negative feelings he felt for the man who held him and the others hostage.

Dr. Sandahl and his team of psychologists were barraged with questions. "My child won't talk about it, yet it seems that he hurts inside. If we ask why, he changes the subject. What should we do?"

"Be supportive and open," they were told. "Let them know they can talk about it freely when they're ready."

"Some of the things I'm hearing from my child are gross and aggressive," said a parent.

"Just listen," was the reply. "Some language or behavior may seem inappropriate for a while. Don't let it shock or disturb you, but broaden your tolerance level to help them work through their feelings."

The children wanted to know if the Youngs were "bad people." "Like machinery, people can sometimes go awry. These people did bad things...."

Said one mother, "My child saw his father pull a rifle out from the truck today and was terrified."

The psychologists knew the reaction well: "Such reminders will initiate fear. This hunting community will have a lot of that."

Another mother said, "My son doesn't really know what

happened. When people talk about it, he isn't sure he knows what happened, and he was there."

Said another, "My daughter says she will never go in Room 4 again."

Counselors from around the country came, wrote or called in to urge the parents just to listen to their children. "Don't even think of what you are going to say next. Simply listen, even if you say nothing." Listening became as natural as breathing. As neighbor listened to neighbor, parent to child, classmate to classmate, love poured in.

School district officials suggested that teachers begin working with therapists the following Tuesday to learn how they could best help the students start school again. It would be vital for teachers to talk through their own problems before helping the kids with theirs. It was decided that counseling would be made available on a walk-in basis and for as long as necessary. "We hesitate to put a time limit on it," officials explained, as each victim works through his fears independently. Counseling would be available, furthermore, to anyone in town. "It is important that no feelings in the community be held in," the psychologists stressed.

Guidelines were taken from a program called Project Cope, provided by the Community Services of the San Diego California Mental Health Department. Five to eleven-year-olds should, the recommendations read, be offered a physical reenactment of the disaster to provide clarification of what had happened. That was one reason school officials made Room 4, still in the condition they had left it on Friday, available to the children and their parents the following Sunday.

The room was open all that day, and except for a tarp thrown on the floor in the room's southwest corner, where Doris's body was found, everything was left untouched. There was even a pair of shoes left behind. Children visiting the room were heard to ask if the owner had been blown right out of them.

Tentatively at first, children with their parents relived the scene inside the blackened room. "This is where I sat," said one.

"I was coloring right here at this desk," pointed out another. They were putting the pieces together in their minds. Some noticed a message scrawled in black on the wall. "Help," it read. Others took time to write their names in the soot. Nearly all the children had asked if they had to return to the hostage site. When they were told no, they went anyway. They didn't want to be there, yet, as one child said, "I had to."

"Re-establishment of ownership is an important part of the healing process," school psychologists told parents and teachers.

Older children were encouraged to talk about the disaster and share their feelings, to rehearse safety measures to be taken in the future, and to express any deep feelings of loss or grieving. School officials told the parents that, as the guidelines predicted, "performance levels in various academic and other skills might drop off for a time—but parents and teachers should reassure the youngsters [that] competency will return."

One important question was when school would resume. Summer vacation was just around the corner. District officials felt that no matter how little work was accomplished in the final days, it was important for the children not to wait three months before returning. At the same time, psychologists felt it necessary to ease students back into school sessions. Students were invited to return when they felt up to it. Most came for a few hours on Wednesday, the first day classes were resumed, then half a day Thursday, and all day Friday, a mere week after the takeover.

On that Wednesday, a few students returned with parents, but most came without them. "More than I expected," said school district counselor Mike Cummings. Cummings and local psychologist George Chournos spent the morning watching children arrive, looking for signs of any problems. "I saw five kids walk up here by themselves real early, and I just about bawled," Chournos said. As one who grew up on a rugged western sheep ranch, Chournos said it struck him that "some of these kids really are tough." He thought the therapy of teachers and children seeing each other again, this time in safe and normal surroundings, "was just as good for the teachers as it was for the children."

Teachers practiced encouraging their students to express whatever was on their minds, he noted later. "Where were you when the bomb went off?" Kliss Sparks asked her fourth graders.

Rusty Birch said he was right next to the lady on fire. "It took me about three seconds to figure out what was going on," he said. "Then I got out of there!"

A key approach to helping everyone leave behind the trauma and begin living normally again was the predictable one of seeking out activities that would reconstruct family and community ties. One such was a Little League Baseball game of "alumni" thirteen-to-fourteen-year-olds against the current nine-to-twelve-year-olds. Because the game was set for Saturday morning, it was nearly canceled. Parents didn't think the kids would be up to it. But the kids voted "yes," and the game was played.

There was an unusual twist to this event. Some of the children had baseball mitts and shoes in the school. Since it was less than a day after the takeover, the police cordon was still in place, sealing off the building. Even though bomb experts had combed the premises for any explosives, detonating them and removing all the weapons to be placed in evidence, investigators were still sifting the entire school property for additional clues needed in any future hearings.

The children were not to go inside. But, hearing that they would need to enter only the north wing, which was nowhere near Room 4, a sympathetic sheriff's deputy listened to their requests. Still, permission was not given.

"Come on, don't you think we've suffered enough," said one of the boys.

The compassionate deputy gave in: "Go get your mitts," he said.

On the following Wednesday, an event of particular importance was held—the annual High School Spring Concert, led by John Miller. There had been speculation that the concert would be canceled because Miller had been injured. His recovery was considered amazingly swift, but everyone wondered if he would be up to conducting an hour-long concert less than a week after being shot near the heart.

"I'm not in pain; I'm glad to be here," he announced to the packed auditorium. It was a simple statement, but it electrified the crowd. They erupted in a spontaneous standing ovation for Miller, for the children, for the teachers. It was also for the entire community. The applause lasted and lasted. People felt they were getting control of their lives again. It felt good to cheer, to whistle, to applaud.

John Miller was known as a quiet, private person who didn't often say much, except through his music. But on this night he wanted to share. A bit hesitant about embarrassing his wife, he proceeded to tell his friends and neighbors how hospital attendants had taken all his clothes in Montpelier and left him with little more than the traditionally-awful, not-so-private, hospital gown. In that garb he was air-lifted to Bannock Memorial Hospital in Pocatello. When the nurse came in to record the valuables that arrived with him, she started at the top and began ticking off the long list of "possibles." John could see it was a very extensive list. "I told her I could save her some time," he said to the crowd. "I have nothing with me but my shorts!"

The audience roared with laughter. When they had

quieted a bit, he added wryly, "Thank goodness for those shorts."

While John was waiting to be taken to the examining room, he was visited by his Episcopal minister, Rev. Lawrence Perry, and the Rev. Gerald Sullivan of Cokeville's Catholic parish. "We would like to give you a blessing," they said.

"I would very much *like* you to give me a blessing," he replied.

"You might say," said Father Sullivan, "that we're the SWAT team for God."

The audience's applause transcended religious boundaries. The room was full of sheer joy. "The healing process is well under way if we can laugh like this," Sherrie Cornia said to the people seated nearby.

The next Friday, Ford Brothers Circus came to town, and Principal Excell, the Mitchells, Rocky Moore and others raced the elephants down Main Street. "Oh, it felt good," a teacher said. "For a time I forgot all about everything." Delighted youngsters cheered for their favorite teacher. At the circus, it was noted that some rides were shunned because the attendants had beards. Mostly, however, it was a particularly happy time.

"It was fun," said one boy, "I ate everything I ever wanted!"

A case of over-indulgence? One father understood the importance of an unfettered good time. "I was happy to give them the opportunity for one night."

Another remarkably positive activity was provided by one

of the Salt Lake City television stations, KUTV. In conjunction with Lagoon Resort, north of Salt Lake City, they put together a special party for all the hostages. It lasted a full summer day, and the station spent thousands of dollars to bus hostages and their families to the amusement park, providing lunch as well. The children soaked up this kind of love— translated into something they could get their hands on. The bumper cars, merry-go-rounds, hot dogs and punch were all additional salve to the wounds received on that bizarre day in mid-May.

Positive activities needed to be accompanied by positive mental attitudes. Some of the adults set the example by saying that they would simply wait out the day when the pain would go away. "Every good thing happens in due time," John Teichert said. Bibles were pulled out and hostages and family members read them together. Scripture reading, uplifting sayings from literature, writing and reading poems—any source of optimism and strength was used as a road map to healing.

Cokeville clergymen counseled their church members to pray that they could purge their memories of hate over this ordeal. LDS Bishop John Teichert pointed out how prayer had "helped from the beginning of this crisis."

At the hospitals, administrators and physicians, prepared for a wave of victims, found most children "highly cheerful," despite painful second and third degree burns. "By golly," said one physician, "their attitude appears to be helping their recovery. I was amazed at how quickly all of the burns I saw healed." Rod Jacobsen, administrator of the Bear Lake Memorial Hospital in Montpelier, said "everyone noticed right away" that the kids were not feeling sorry for themselves or harboring self-pity. "They just wanted to do what had to be done."

Nine days after the bomb exploded, Gina Taylor, who came near to losing her eye in the blast, participated in a church program where her father spoke. As she sang "I Am a Child of God," she was able to watch the audience with both eyes. They could see only a little white patch on her face where she had been burned. "Lead me, guide me, walk beside me. Help me find the way," came the words. Perhaps they had never been felt as deeply.

In time, doctors said that only a few victims would carry permanent scars, or have long months of slow recovery, like Billie Jo Hutchinson would. "That in itself is something of a miracle," said one parent, "judging from what the doctors first feared."

Many people did not want the unique aspects of their escape to be forgotten. Said one woman, "I think this should be remembered as a miracle of the same magnitude as the parting of the Red Sea."

One of the most memorable comments was made by Tina Cook: "Deep down I don't want to ever forget how bad this was because I don't want to ever forget how good it eventually turned out either."

The town itself took an action that further underscored its independence and ability to recover—it politely refused state aid. "The town is so self-sufficient," said Audrey Cotherman, of Wyoming's Department of Education, "that it has not needed state aid and has done very well on its own resources. Cokeville is the most remarkable community we've ever seen. Those people responded and organized themselves. I cannot praise the community enough."

In their efforts to heal themselves and their children and neighbors, the citizens had to move through one of the most difficult but important steps of recovery, forgiving themselves and others. As the town pulled tightly together, it seemed for a time that one person was virtually forgotten. She was the only person in the entire community who had lost a loved one—Bernie Petersen, Doris Young's daughter.

Not only had she lost her mother, she was afraid she had also lost her friends. At first, she was merely shocked. "My own mother doing something like that? I kept asking myself why she would endanger children's lives that way. Could I have stopped her? I felt guilty—but I had no idea. We loved living here in Cokeville," she explained. "My husband was born and raised here. This is his home."

Some people in town had to work through the animosity in their own minds. It was difficult for them to be reminded of the horror they experienced at the hands of David and Doris. Some neighbors just didn't know what to say to the Petersens. The first to find the words were the Morfelds, parents of one of the most seriously burned children, Tina. Bernie was assured they did not blame her for what happened. More encouraged, the Petersens wrestled with their feelings. Then they decided to stay.

In one of the many ironies of the takeover, that which had lured David to town in the first place—its strong family ties—now began to mitigate and dissipate what he had planned. David had been defeated by the very love and unity which he believed was Cokeville's weakest point. He had manipulated that love to take control; now his victims were allowing it to come in, and learning how to use it to walk free of his memory.

An editorial in the Salt Lake City *Deseret News*, one week after the incident, contained this comment: "If a lesson emerges from this episode, it is a lesson about what can happen to individuals who start nursing a grievance, real or imagined—who convince themselves they are right and everyone else is wrong.... As was so graphically demonstrated by the Cokeville madness, people can poison themselves with their own ideas."

Among the many letters from throughout the nation was one from a retired elementary teacher in a rural South Dakota town. Her words aptly expressed the truths learned by the children and parents of Cokeville, as they moved away from their ordeal and back toward real life: "Fear is a counterfeit of faith. When we put faith to work, it will always overcome fear. Love always overcomes hate. The counterfeit of anything is never as powerful as the real thing."

Life will not be taken for granted in Cokeville as casually as before. Its preciousness is too highly valued. There is more understanding and more compassion now. Had David Gary

Young understood such emotions, he might never have done what he did.

Chapter Six
PROBING FOR ANSWERS

"David and Doris Young could have each received a minimum of 3,080 years in prison for the kidnapping charges alone."
—*Lincoln County Attorney Richard Leonard*

O ut in the larger world, Cokeville's near-catastrophe became a "nine-days' wonder." Media representatives from the region began descending on the town before the hostages were barely out of the building. Their counterparts from all over the nation, and from foreign press bureaus, made some kind of contact, pushing coverage of world events temporarily aside in the powerful human interest generated by the siege of the elementary school. In addition to coping with physical injuries and psychological traumas, suffered in their confrontation with David Young, the hostages and their friends and families would have to cope with the sometimes-enlightening and sometimes-intrusive inquiries of the press and the massive official investigation.

The *Salt Lake Tribune*, with a next-morning deadline and very little time to act, kept its coverage succinct, capturing the essence of the ordeal in its May 17 lead: "Terror by bomb and gunfire tore through an elementary school Friday...."

The next day, with more time to assess what happened, the newspaper reported: "Aftermath of Explosion 'a Miracle.'"

Salt Lake City TV station KUTV did such an excellent job of early coverage that their reports were picked up by a London TV network. In London, American Stuart Wilson, who had lived in Utah, was startled to see news of a town he knew. KUTV had been so timely, in fact, that their arrival on the scene minutes before the bomb went off evoked semi-serious jokes about "being notified by the Youngs in advance." Part of the legal investigation centered for a time on whether David Young had given someone in the press notification so he could air his political views.

What really happened was that KUTV had a crew in the tri-state area on another assignment. They did not have their portable relay equipment along, but they managed to get footage of children, at the moment of their escape, embracing parents in a reunion which was the envy of every other television station.

Not all the coverage was this pertinent and accurate. In fact, errors in reporting the story seemed to be the rule rather than the exception. An article in *Time* magazine, printed the week following the takeover, managed to incorporate over 30 errors of fact or distortion in its pages. David Young was described as an "orphan obsessed with guns." He may have been obsessed with guns, but he was not an orphan. The article reported that he had "returned" to Cokeville "with a terrible vengeance," implying that grievances at not being permanently hired after his six-months' probation period as marshal ended were the origin of his plan to take over the school.

In describing the initial phase of the takeover, the article stated that "...Young and his wife Doris, 47, calmly unloaded three gasoline bombs, nine handguns and four rifles." There had been only one bomb, and the number of handguns was inflated. David wore three visible guns; a fourth was hidden in his belt at the back and Doris had a gun in her purse. According to the *Time* article, the hostages "stood at gun point in frightened silence," but they were not required to stand and David did permit conversation. Although the guns were certainly present and certainly used to keep the group under control, David did not have the hostages "at gun point" throughout the whole afternoon. He apparently raised a gun at them only when he felt their obedience needed to be reemphasized.

"Declaring that he had enough explosives to 'wipe out Cokeville,'" the article continued, "Young told Principal Max Excell that he wanted...[to] talk with President Reagan." David had claimed that the bomb could "wipe out the entire school," not the town; he never asked to speak to President Reagan, Excell said.

This particular error was picked up and even compounded by the *Denver Post* and several other newspapers, who said that David had forced one or more of the hostages to call President Reagan and/or threaten the government. David had indeed sent his "Zero Equals Infinity" paper to the president, but made no attempt to call him during the siege.

Principal Excell tried to correct the error, stating: "No, I was never at any time during the crisis directed to call the president as some media reported. And I was the only one allowed on the school telephone." In an interview on the 19th of May, he elaborated: "No one could be certain, in the chaos and confusion of the afternoon, what actually did take place. Bomb experts and sheriff's deputies sifted evidence and reached few concrete conclusions until late the first day, and in some cases, the second day. It seemed the media made up things to fill in gaps in their stories."

The *Time* article continued with statements that were near the mark but far enough off to be both misleading and irritating. "As police surrounded the school and townspeople scrambled to raise ransom money," read the article, "Doris tried to comfort the scared and tired children by bringing in library books, crayons and television set." The school was never surrounded. Townspeople never attempted to raise the ransom money (which would have been impossible, had they even tried to do so—the town had no bank and the total request was $2 million per child, $270 million dollars at least, even if adult hostages were left out of the calculations.) Finally, it was the teachers who asked and got permission to provide the necessary diversions for the children, not Doris Young.

Covering the end of the siege, the article said: "After a 2 1/2 hour standoff, Young left to go to the bathroom, handing his wife, who was standing in the center of the room, two bottles of gasoline wired to a battery and manual trigger." Doris was not handed anything which she had to juggle while keeping track of an easily-tripped trigger; there was only one bottle of gasoline and it was on the shopping cart. The exchange between David and Doris was only to untie the shoelace-trigger from David's wrist and retie it on Doris's.

"When her hand apparently slipped on the trigger," the report explained, "she set off the crude bomb." This is at odds with hostage reports that she raised her hand too far and overreached the trigger's safety margin, probably inadvertently. Further, the bomb was considered complicated, not crude, by experts who examined it. "The blast killed her instantly," the writer asserted dramatically— but it didn't. The autopsy would show a different cause of death.

The escape was described in these words: "Reeling teachers shoved children through the blown-out windows onto the grass outside, where they lay screaming and shivering with shock as their parents fought through police lines to reach them." None of the windows was blown out; the large window was later broken by firefighters and EMT personnel in an effort to make their assault on the fire more swift and effective. While the children were certainly making noise (as were the adults), the "screaming and shivering" phrase leaves the wrong impression on the reader. Some children ran to the waiting crowd immediately on escaping through the window. Others responded immediately when Rocky Moore told them to get up and run; it was also an overstatement to say that the parents were fighting through police lines. Law officers simply held parents back for their own good when the bomb exploded; as children ran from the schoolroom, police stepped out of the way. At no time was there a violent confrontation between parents and police, as the phrasing of the *Time* article would imply.

Of the aftermath, the article stated: "Some 70 people were later hospitalized; at least one child had burns over 50% of his body." The total number of 79 was arrived at after counting and recounting—a not serious reporting error of nine persons. (One media report from a different source had only 40 people being treated in area hospitals.) But, the "one child" referred to in the article was a girl, Billie Jo Hutchinson, not a boy, and the damage was 21%, not 50%, of her body, fully severe enough to threaten her life.

The music teacher's injury was also inaccurately reported in the *Time* article: "Young, rushing back from the toilet, shot school band leader Jon Miller, wounding him in the back." Miller's first name is spelled "John," and he was moving toward the door to leave the room when he came upon David, who was standing in the doorway of the restroom. Miller thus approached David (unexpectedly); David didn't rush up to John Miller.

Eva Clark, six of whose children were hostage with her, said on May 17, 1986, that the *Time* account did not happen as written. Her first-hand experience of David Young gave her the right to be a little scornful of the big-time magazine assuming to interpret for the nation the goings-on in her small town. "Who makes this stuff up?" she asked bluntly, and further noted: "Media guessed at some events I knew to be false. Some information could have been obtained by asking a single question at Town Hall, or even of my child who was at the hostage scene. But the reporter never asked any of the eye-witnesses here what they had seen."

The errors, both big and little, piled up. The *Arizona Daily Star* and several newspapers described Doris as wearing a blue blouse; witnesses said it was red. All the media initially reported money as a motive for the takeover and, in general, did not correct their stories when other motives were soon added to the list.

Said Sheriff's Deputy Ron Hartley, "Money couldn't be the primary reason. There was no getaway vehicle and no way the perpetrators could carry any money from the crime scene. Money would obviously not do the perpetrators much good if they couldn't escape with it; so we began to check the diaries and journals for the real reason for taking the hostages. We found statements that [indicated] we were dealing with 'crazies' who struck the town because it was a 'family town' with lots of children. The pair apparently sought to kill these school children, get them away from 'corrupt' school and government administrators and be a ruler over the children in another world. As bizarre as it was, that appears [to be] the real motive."

The *Las Vegas Sun*, in a report later picked up by the *New York Times*, stated that the perpetrators had "acted in collusion with other dangerous groups still at large." The *Sun* headline read: "Mad Bombers linked to tax radicals," with subhead, "Ransom sought to fund Posse Comitatus Revolt." (The fundamental concept behind Posse Comitatus is that locally-determined laws supersede all other laws, particularly federal regulations and jurisdictions). The story said that even though the two perpetrators were dead, U.S. schools and government were likely endangered by their still-living colleagues throughout America.

The only possible source for such a connection was a few lines in David Young's diary which merely mentioned basics of the Posse Comitatus idea. The story about the hostage-takers being in collusion with a group plotting to overthrow the U.S. Government was never supported by any actual evidence provided by any news-gatherer (or anyone else) at the time of the official investigation, nor has any come to light in the years since the hostage incident.

"There is nothing to indicate veracity of the Sun statement," said Lincoln County Sheriff's Deputy Ron Hartley, who made an extensive study of the perpetrators' many journals and diaries. "There was never any hint of the Youngs being in conspiracy with a Posse Comitatus group, only an isolated mention of the Posse idea. The Youngs were clearly 'loners' and when they died, their bizarre and dangerous scheme died with them."

Lincoln County Sheriff T. Deb Wolfley seconded Hartley's opinion: "Perhaps it made a good story. But there was just never anything to support the collusion idea. Every piece of evidence gathered pointed to this man and wife team, David and Doris Young, not communicating or cooperating with others on anything they did. All evidence points to them acting entirely on their own."

The most irresponsible reporting was the teletype message received by a radio station in Rexburg, Idaho. An employee there telephoned to Principal Excell's son, Steve, that when the bomb detonated, "everyone in the building was killed." Knowing Steve was from Cokeville, the caller said, "I knew you would want to know."

"Did you know my dad and little sister were in that building?" Steve asked. While Steve was dealing with the agonizing news, the phone rang again. This time it was his mother calling from Cokeville, informing him that all the hostages escaped. The confusion was devastating and unnecessary.

There was insensitive behavior as well as irresponsible behavior on the part of some media people: one newsman called Principal Excell in the middle of the night for an early morning appointment at the schoolhouse, and then did not show up on time. Small errors occurred in many of the reports, not crucial to the core of the story but very irritating to those who were part of it. Cokeville was incorrectly located on some maps; names were misspelled, such as "Jon" Miller and "Dorris" Young; the population of Cokeville was inaccurately reported.

Townspeople said some reporters hurried to a telephone within minutes of arrival to call in a story before the "facts" they were reporting were verified either by hostages or by lawmen—then caught a private plane out of town the same afternoon.

Genera Robinson, who lived adjacent to the school, said in an interview on the 19th of May: "It seemed to my family and me that the reporter [calling on our telephone] could not possibly know what was going on inside the hostage-taken school building; yet, the reporter reported as fact what no one yet knew. Things like precisely how the children were being threatened, adults cringing in fear." No one knew what was happening inside that building until eye-witnesses eluded the hostage-takers and told their stories to police. By then, many reporters had gone home.

Some of the many media mistakes can be accepted as honest oversights, made while reporters hurried to meet deadlines which took no cognizance of the realities operating in the town itself or the lives of the hostages. Yet the presence of really serious errors of fact and interpretation raises the possibility that media people had run a very broad gamut in covering the Cokeville takeover, including at least four levels of inferior journalism: (1) careless data-gathering, (2) guesswork, (3) deliberate exaggeration for the sake of sensationalizing the story, and/or (4) outright fabrication.

To be fair to all news representatives, the story was a dramatic and confusing one in a remote area, with few quick and simple answers. News unfolded inside, while reporters waited outside. News people at the scene also had to deal with the fact that the event occurred late in the afternoon, leaving scant room to prepare copy, with press deadlines a few hours away, in time for the morning edition.

There was, fortunately, press coverage both sensitive to the feelings of people in the town and accurate to the story itself. Here are a few "sound bite" examples from different media organizations:

Carol Mikita, KSL-TV, Salt Lake City: "It is a story of tragedy and twisted thinking...."

Greg Lefevere, CNN, Atlanta: "A town of miracles? That could be right. A third of the town was being held hostage...strong family ties pulled them through."

Charlene Brown, KUTV, quoting one of the hostage schoolgirls, referring to Doris and David Young: "She was a nice lady but the guy sounded like he was going to kill everybody."

Bomb expert Richard Haskell, interviewed on CNN: "The false ceiling absorbed much of the bomb blast. I can't express how fortunate they are. It's unreal...so fortunate. You look in there and wonder why there aren't 150 kids lying in there dead."

One article perceived by the eye-witnesses as particularly error-free was that published in *U.S. News and World Report* which came out about two weeks after the incident. The article contained the photograph of a small child peering into the school room which had been such a scene of terror several days before. The caption read: "Inch by Inch." Both article and picture received high acclaim from hostages and eye-witnesses to the incident, who felt it captured not only the facts of the story but the poignancy as well.

One of the first to fully comprehend the significance of David Young's diaries was the Salt Lake City *Deseret News.* In a copyrighted story dated May 31 (13 days after the fact, which gave them sufficient time to research the accuracy of their statements) the newspaper said: "Investigators now believe the 'Biggie' was much bigger—and more horrible—than at first suspected. Young's writing indicates he was planning on...a place where he would rule as God of a new race, a place that could only be reached through death. The ramifications are...terrible."

Some newsmen asked the pertinent, difficult questions: "What will be the psychological effect on the children?" Other questions were easier to deal with: "How will this event be handled by the children at school on the first anniversary?" Consulting the calendar, someone determined it to be a Saturday. "Thank goodness for that," one teacher said.

Absent from most of the reports were criticisms of the way lawmen, volunteers, hostages, or others reacted during and after the incident. Usually when such extreme stresses are introduced into any community or situation, it precipitates a chain reaction of human weaknesses, aggravating further tensions. Given the outcome of this particular incident—no lawsuits or official complaints—there seemed to be no one who actually deserved criticism. This was highly unusual for a story with such negative beginnings.

The best story about the press itself was probably that running in the *Star Valley* (Wyoming) *Independent*, written by

Cokeville correspondent Gwen Petersen. The headline was, "Cokeville bombed with news media." "It's been a new experience for most of the people of Cokeville to be so closely associated with the news media," the article ran. "Television cameras were on the scene shortly after the bombing tragedy occurred and have stayed throughout the week. A satellite truck transmitting live coverage has parked near the elementary school, and anyone walking down the street has been subject to an interview. Residents have opened their homes to newsmen, providing telephone service for calls all over the country. Principal Max Excell received calls from San Francisco radio stations and the *Sunday Today* newspaper from London, and he was interviewed by the three major national networks, plus the *Washington Post, Denver Post,* AP and UPI wire services out of Washington, and countless others who were on the scene. The incident has received excellent coverage from the media. The people of Cokeville are now looking forward to the time when the news people will leave so they can go on with their lives."

To handle the invasion of the press, the Lincoln County Sheriff's Office set up a media information center immediately following the hostage takeover. They realized, as the scope of the incident became clear, through the reports of both Principal Excell and David Young's daughter, Princess, that media involvement was totally unavoidable, and must therefore be coordinated so as not to conflict with the official investigation.

Hostages were busy trying to find answers to questions. Jean Mitchell wanted to know why the buses hadn't arrived on time but grateful they hadn't. She learned that Principal Excell had told the drivers to stay away. If they had been heard outside the besieged school room, students might have bolted for the doors.

Within fifteen minutes after the bomb exploded in Cokeville, Lincoln County Assistant Attorney Richard Leonard was at the schoolhouse to provide legal advice, including questions of proper search warrant and investigative procedure. He would help to initiate the most monumental criminal investigation in the county's history. The takeover, in Leonard's own words, "appeared to us to be the most extensive act of terrorism ever attempted in the United States."

Along with Leonard, County Sheriff's Investigators Earl Carroll and Ron Hartley spent days in the schoolroom, talked to hostages, and pored over evidence in the case. All were veterans at their jobs. Leonard had spent more than five years in the attorney's office, while Carroll had been a police chief in Utah for twelve years before joining Lincoln County. Hartley had also spent years with the county as an investigative officer. Together, they launched a thorough probe into everything known about David and Doris Young: their possessions, travels, lifestyle, and particularly their diaries.

Standard legal procedure dictates that the first person on the scene is the "controlling officer." It was difficult to determine here who should be considered the "first." Deputy Carroll was the first to arrive in Cokeville, while Deputy Randy White was the first to discover David Young's body. With the passage of time, various aspects of the investigation were given to various lawmen. Earl Carroll was initially put in charge; more specific assignments were made as time went on.

When Deputy Ron Hartley arrived in Cokeville, he had heard nothing of the crisis on his car radio, and assumed a "massive mock drill" was in progress. He was soon told otherwise and taken inside the school building. Later, the forty-one diaries and journals of David and Doris that had been located were turned over to Hartley, who began the complicated process of examining them, both for a basic understanding of the two personalities, and for specific references to the "Biggie" of May 16, 1986.

While the siege was under way, but prior to the explosion, two agents from the Federal Bureau of Investigation in Boise and Denver were hurrying to Cokeville to help negotiate the ransom. To be more accurate, they were hoping to talk the Youngs out of their extortion threats. When the bomb exploded, that wasn't necessary anymore. But they were still involved because it is a federal crime to kidnap or attempt to kidnap anyone. Agents from the Federal Bureau of Alcohol, Tobacco and Firearms were also enroute, pulled in by David Young's weapons violations.

In the matter of weapons, investigators turned up three guns the hostages didn't know the Youngs had. One of them

was a .22 caliber pistol Doris carried in her purse. Another
was the .22 caliber pistol David had tucked in the back of his
trousers. In all that made four guns on his person. Still
another firearm the hostages didn't see was the .44 caliber
Bulldog pistol found in the restroom with Young's body.

In some news accounts, a .44 Magnum was mentioned as
one of the weapons used at the school by Young. If so, he
returned it to the hallway. Law officers found it there later
alongside an AR-15 semi-automatic, a shotgun and 30
blasting caps (identified as "bombs" in some media
coverage). Some of the confiscated rifles carried scopes,
normally used for long-range outdoor, not indoor, shooting.
Why did David bring them? Were they an indication he
intended to leave with live hostages, and the scopes were for
sighting on lawmen he expected to be pursued by? There
were no answers—the scopes were simply another anomaly
turned up by the investigation, as were the additional bomb
wires and more guns than the Youngs could use.

It was later conjectured by Deputy Hartley that these were
Young's prized possessions he intended to take with him to
his reincarnated Brave New World.

Lawmen found stores of gunpowder and ammunition,
and expected to find more guns, in the Young's Tucson
mobile home. They feared booby traps, according to the
Pima County Sheriff's Office, but fortunately found none.
Other bomb components and weapons were found in the
Montpelier motel where the Youngs stayed before the
takeover. In Tucson, they also found a note from Doris to

Princess, inviting her to take whatever of Doris's jewelry she wanted. "To remember me by," the note concluded.

One of the central issues needing to be resolved, for legal determinations required before the case could be closed, was the question of how David and Doris died. The answer seemed obvious, but it had to be established officially and precisely. Even to confirm what was already assumed, painstaking investigative procedures had to be followed. Members of the ATF force helped in this determination. Wearing their yellow coats with the large black "ATF" stenciled on the back, they were very much a part of the scene. The investigation concluded that David had shot his wife after she caught fire from the explosion.

Earl Carroll said that David used the .44 Bulldog to shoot Doris. David fired two slugs, one of which missed her; the other killed her. One of the slugs, presumably the one which missed her entirely, was found in the ceiling tile. The other slug remained in her body. Lawmen concluded that David must have been shooting upward from a low angle in the smoke-filled room. Although unlikely, he may not have known who she was, but simply fired at a figure moving toward him.

Some of the investigators were displeased that Doris's body had been removed from the blood-spotted southwest corner of the room where she apparently died. Moving a body from its crime scene always negatively impacts an investigation—evidence can too easily be shifted, destroyed or otherwise compromised. The EMTs explained, however, that they thought they were removing an adult hostage who might respond to mouth-to-mouth resuscitation. It was an understandable judgment call, made in the midst of physical danger, and without the luxury of time to ponder all possible consequences.

Just before shooting Doris, David came face to face with John Miller and shot him. He then came face to face with Eva Clark and her children, and did not shoot. Very soon thereafter, he shot his wife; seconds later he went back to the restroom, placed the .45 caliber Colt beneath his chin and pulled the trigger. When Sheriff's Deputy Randy White discovered David's body, he followed proper legal procedure in leaving it precisely where it was. He moved it only slightly, when he put handcuffs on, immediately after finding David, just in case he wasn't actually dead. The body remained where it was lying, and in the same position, until some four hours later when Lincoln County Coroner Michael Richins arrived. Carroll said that the gun David used to kill himself was apparently his favorite, a custom-made weapon bearing the serial number "DGY-1" ("David Gary Young, Number One").

David's body was removed to the Kemmerer City Morgue. Dr. William Fogarty, medical examiner for the state of Wyoming, traveled from Jackson to perform the autopsy. No sign of drug use, including marijuana or significant alcoholic intake, was found. It was determined he had taken a few beers on the day he died, Sheriff Wolfley said.

One of the facts to be determined before the body was

turned over to relatives was whether Young had, indeed, committed suicide. County Attorney Richard Leonard noted there are many ways to determine whether someone has shot himself. One is the angle of the cartridge entry, another is powder burns from firing at close range. Based on these factors, the county officially determined that David had taken his own life. This confirmed the suspicions of those who had discovered and removed the body.

The body was then turned over to relatives, including Princess, and taken by them to the Crandall Mortuary in Evanston. Princess, after being questioned, exonerated and released, was allowed to leave the area. Her fiancé drove up from Tucson to take her back with him.

Doris's body was turned over to Bernie Petersen and family members.

Little was ever said about one phase of the investigation: the recruitment of area teenagers to help comb the school grounds. They searched it inch-by-inch for "anything which appeared to be out of kilter" with what was there before the Youngs arrived. Every discolored or burned shred of paper, blade of grass, or unaccounted flotsam, anything and everything, was flagged with a pink marker on a wire stick. Some of the items could well have been left by kids during recess or lunch hour or have fallen from pockets of firemen and EMTs running toward the smoldering classroom. With hundreds of wires piercing the grounds, the yard soon resembled a giant pin cushion.

One of the most frustrating aspects of the investigation

was the attempt to determine exactly why David left the main classroom for the restroom. His autopsy confirmed that the reason did not have to do with his diabetic condition: he did not have his insulin supplies on his person when he left for the bathroom, and none was found in the room itself. (His supply was still out in the hall.) Further, he appeared to be having no problems with thirst or pressure to urinate. Some witnesses, but not all, said David was beginning to "sweat profusely." What, if anything, that had to do with leaving the room is not known. There was no pathological indication that his blood was diabetically imbalanced.

If his physical illness did not cause him to leave the classroom, what did? All the other hypotheses focused on his state of mind, and there could be no exact determination of that, only reasonably logical speculation. Hostage accounts of how long he stayed in the restroom were inconsistent, so it would not be safe to base a conjecture solely on the premise that he was "hiding" or "withdrawing."

Hostages knew that David initially expected, or at least wanted them to believe he expected, to hold the children ten or more days, yet there was no indication he had prepared effectively for that long a stay, except for one statement that they could send out for food. He had provided no bedding for himself or Doris, let alone for the hostages. Nor did he seem to be prepared for night vigils when either he or his wife would have to stay awake. Did he realize at some point that he hadn't made the crucial preparations he thought he had made? The hostages became convinced that something did cause him to become tense and anxious as the afternoon wore on. They felt this something mount until it became more than David Young could handle.

The perplexing question raises an even more fundamental one about the nature of David Young himself. This was a man who was known for his methodical rejection of emotionalism, a man whose life was, if the diaries are to be believed, making practical plans for an eternal existence that would bridge the abyss between this life and the next, and leave him successful and triumphant, finished with the petty whinings of common people who couldn't understand him and the obstructions of official people who were only standing in his way. He certainly saw himself as a disciplined and superior thinker who left nothing to chance. Yet the plan to take the Cokeville Elementary School hostage was filled with inconsistencies, seeming errors of judgment and unbalanced emotional responses to his colleagues.

For instance, the discrepancy between the threat of ten days' siege and the reality of no visible preparations for that long a standoff has already been mentioned. He told the children they were not to use the water fountain or the restroom. Did he forget the complete impossibility of anyone complying with those rules over a ten-day span? Or did he already know that the takeover period would be far shorter than the time span he implied to his victims?

Why did David, with a reputation for being so meticulous, wait so long to obtain the gasoline container? Whether he found his jug at the Cokeville dump or brought one with him from the brief stay in Montpelier, how could he fail to notice the leak in it? And why did he choose such a complicated explosive device requiring substantial labor to wire together correctly? It was certainly a visible threat to the hostages and helped keep them cowed and obedient; it was also bulky, cumbersome and dangerous to drag around.

Why did he react as he did to Princess's outburst, not merely letting her leave with his only means of escape, but actually throwing the van keys at her, knowing that she would be free to contact authorities, if she chose, almost before he could effectively secure the building?

Why did he disdain human companionship and normal social interaction, for the most part, and yet try to gather around him, for the perpetration of his one great masterstroke, a set of colleagues including a cousin, a business investor and a former co-worker, as well as his wife and daughter? The "fun and games" reference made in his diary just prior to the takeover attempt seems almost ludicrously at odds with his much more frequent and well-documented preference for self-isolation and disdain.

And why did a man who apparently so carefully oversaw every facet of the hostage takeover, abruptly leave it all to his wife and disappear into the restroom? None of the hostages report his giving Doris any instructions or even having any real conversation with her before he changed the trigger string from his hand to hers. He just did so, and left. Perhaps it was merely to go to the bathroom, as seemed obvious, and the sense some of the hostages had of his taking a long time was a factor of the pressure they were under and the looming nature of each second that passed. When the bomb exploded moments later, it took any certainty with it. The hostages would never be sure; the investigators would not be able to determine David's exact intentions.

Perhaps one key to solving this puzzle is the knowledge that David consistently acted for his own best interests, regardless of the outcome for others. A relative who talked to Cokeville Mayor Dayton about David's refusal to end his habit of taking and selling nude photos at every opportunity, even among family members, made a sad, insightful comment about the dead kidnapper: "He just did anything he wanted and thought he could get away with it. Too often he did."

The diaries reveal that David simply didn't perceive the will or choice of anyone else to be as valid as his own. Investigator Ron Hartley said that he determined, after months of intense scrutiny of the diaries, that David specifically sought children of high intelligence to take with him into his "Brave New World" of reincarnation. "It was clear in Young's writings that he had an obsession with starting a new world with pliable and intelligent young minds." In writing, David could dismiss the problem of having to terrorize the beneficiaries of his superior intellect to get to that world, and ignore that leaving behind him a trail of broken families and unbearable losses should have shaken his faith in the rightness of what he was doing. It seems certain that he not only didn't, but couldn't, consider other people's needs and feelings. Life and death had lost the shapes and relationships they have for most people on the planet.

Earl Carroll reiterated what other investigators had said about Young's intentions. "It doesn't appear from all the evidence that David Young ever planned on walking from the school building alive."

By an early age, his intellect and ego were little tempered by any overt compassion for others. With few social contacts, there was not much opportunity to determine how far out of line he might have been with the rest of the world. He was dangerous because of a fanatical compulsion to prove that he was always right. In retrospect, it may be why he committed suicide—he could not bear to be told that he was not only wrong in what he did, but incompetent as well. He may not have been brave enough to face the disapproval of those he felt were inferior to himself. If so, that is itself ironic, since his proclaimed intention was to take his hostages into a "brave new world."

There is another psychological key, dredged up from the diaries, that may prove equally useful in revealing how David Young reached so ambitiously for a reality he couldn't find, and failed to recognize the reality that surrounded him. It is a subjective view of the man, but one which supports the hostage accounts of his temperament during the siege. His mind seems to have taken him into more than a mere wrestling match with logic. Life may have become more and more bitter, as he faced the ugly realization that his profound conclusions had not brought him any meaningful satisfaction. Life was as empty after his years of pondering as it had been when he was young. He had all the intellectual answers now, but where was his reward for the years of enormous effort?

If, as many believe, his thought processes operated in a vacuum of positive emotions, his ability to process day-to-day communication, the emotional giving and receiving between humans, may have been disintegrating in the last years of pamphlet-writing and planning his other-worldly "Biggie." The possibility being considered here is that the tensions of the takeover situation itself finally drained his resources, leaving him with nothing to recharge the human spirit, even a withdrawn and unbalanced spirit like his, with enough desire or stamina to carry out its own long-dreamed-of scheme.

County Attorney Richard Leonard, having to deal with the realities David Young rejected, stated that his office was prepared to charge both David and Doris with kidnapping, if they had lived. If convicted of that crime alone, each could have received a minimum of 20 years for each of the 154 hostages. That would have added up to 3,080 years for each of them. And since the penalty for kidnapping is 20 years to life, it could have been even longer. "Their sentences would also have been consecutive, not concurrent," Leonard emphasized. Further, David and Doris would have been charged equally as co-conspirators in the kidnapping. Had David lived, he would have faced a first degree murder charge in the death of his wife, and would also have been charged with attempted murder in the first degree for shooting John Miller.

Under the definition of felony kidnapping, it is not necessary, as Richard Leonard noted, to transport victims anywhere for the crime of kidnapping or hostage-taking to occur. Threats against a person to hold him or her anywhere are sufficient for the crime to be charged, Leonard explained; "In this case it happened within the school classroom." Since a review in 1932 of the famous Lindbergh kidnapping case, the crime of kidnapping was made a federal offense, allowing the involvement of the FBI, if the victim were transported across state lines. In 1956 the law was strengthened to be applicable as a federal offense, twenty-four hours after a kidnapping, whether the victim was transported or not.

While David's shooting of Doris in her fiery hysteria may have been considered by some to be a mercy killing, as far as Lincoln County was concerned, it was first degree murder. In Doris's case, the "felony rule" applied: during the commission of a felony, if anyone is killed, whether it be a criminal accomplice, intended victim, or innocent bystander, the perpetrator of the felony is liable for first-degree murder charges. Thus, since the autopsy confirmed Doris had died of a bullet wound and not of the effects of the fire, David was doubly responsible for her death: both by bringing a bomb threat into the school, and through shooting her while the felony siege was occurring.

Even had Doris not been injured or killed, there would

likely have been no lenience for her. She entered the school building on her own volition, without any known coercion from her husband. On the other hand, Richard Leonard said that Princess would probably not have been charged—even, possibly, if she had remained with her father in the school room—due to the fact that her life was once threatened. Deppe and Mendenhall, handcuffed in the back of the van, were clearly not part of the kidnapping-extortion scheme, once they realized what David intended to involve them in. At least this was the thinking of the county. Carroll made it clear that the federal government has the prerogative to reach its own conclusions in cases such as this.

Some people were curious as to whether David and/or Doris could ever have been found innocent by reason of insanity, and then released later from a mental institution, once they were declared cured. Said Leonard: "That is slim in this case. But you have to say it is always a possibility. I can't speak for a judge or jury." There was, however, a great deal of information available to a jury which they could have used to reach a just verdict. These sources include tapes made of conversations between Cokeville Town Hall and Principal Excell in the school during the takeover; tapes with lawmen and emergency vehicles; and depositions taken from school teachers among the hostage group.

All this information added up, by late autumn of 1986, to what Carroll labeled as "a report more than four inches thick." He also said that, in an unusual move, the report was copyrighted to prevent unauthorized use of any part of it until released for public access, the precise time unknown.

One positive law enforcement gain that emerged from the Cokeville incident was the long-awaited Lincoln County SWAT team, organized in the months that followed. The team received special training by FBI agents concerning bombs, weapons, and tactical methods for dealing with terrorists.

As life returned to normal, the Lincoln County School District drew up several resolutions praising hostages for doing everything they could to prevent matters from becoming worse. They assured Tina Cook and others that there was really nothing anyone could have done to prevent the Youngs from entering the Cokeville Elementary School on May 16, 1986. Such statements helped assuage feelings of guilt that some of the school officials naturally felt after the extortion assault.

What about additional "more realistic" fire drills? Would they help children better prepare for future crises? Certainly, the Youngs' crime was unusual, but just as a precaution, "more drills from a single room in case of fire or emergency" were decided upon. Cokeville school officials were always convinced by the ordeal's aftermath that the fire drill conducted from the school cafeteria the week before helped the children get clear of the room with less panic and confusion.

It is noteworthy that, in that practice drill, no one had to exit through a window. The window in Room 4 measures 13 1/2 inches high and 28 1/2 inches wide. It opens at an angle, allowing only a ten-inch clearance from sill to frame. Yet, it is estimated that 70% of the 154 hostages made their escape that way. And this in the thirty to forty-five seconds estimated by sheriff's deputies after interviewing eyewitnesses.

Richard Leonard concluded, "I've seen it all; homicides, drug busts, all kinds of things among crimes and criminals. Yet I have never seen anything as potentially lethal and dangerous turn out so positively for so many innocent people.... It seemed even more so the deeper we probed into the Youngs, their many writings, and into the many depositions that we have gathered." Continuing, he said: "There are many unanswered questions. From looking over all the facts, I simply cannot see how all of the hostages got out alive."

In a letter written October 27, 1986, Earl Carroll stated that the "case is not closed out, and the possibility of future prosecutions has not been ruled out. The case has been referred to the United States Dept. of Justice and is being reviewed." But by February 5, 1987, the *Star Valley Independent* published the news that the official investigation of the Cokeville hostage incident had finally been completed. The paper cited Sheriff Wolfley's report that the "investigators have reviewed the case with the Lincoln County Attorney's Office, U.S. Attorney's Office and the Department of Justice and that the case is now closed."

After the intensity of the ordeal and the remarkable outcome which the entire town had experienced, Cokeville was ready to rejoin the world it had known before David

Young invaded it.

His philosophy, that "knowledge is all we have and knowledge is nothing," overlooked the more important understanding that love for one another can transcend all else. That oversight probably cost the Youngs their revolution and their lives.

Love for one another was now breathing life back into this entire community. These citizens who were working to exhibit that love described it as a product of their faith in prayer and Deity.

May 16, 1986, will always remind citizens of Cokeville of unhappy memories. They will also remember it, perhaps even more vividly, as a time of overcoming adversity, a memory of the human values exemplified by mind, heart and spirit...a time when they talk of a power beyond their own that heard—and answered—their prayers.

What They're Doing Now

As of April 3, 1994, nearly every burn victim has fully recovered. Pat Bennion, the substitute teacher badly injured helping children from the inferno in Room 4, is fully recuperated. One who is not is Billie Jo Hutchinson, still undergoing operations for burns to the face. Verlene Bennion, 66 at the time of the hostage crisis, who suffered from prolonged smoke inhalation, has returned to normal.

John Miller, the music teacher shot by David Young, still carries the .22 slug eight years later. (Doctors said the slug was too close to his heart to operate.) He is now "going strong" as a music teacher in Powell, Wyoming, and says he feels "no ill effects."

All of the faculty at the Cokeville Elementary School remain except for Max Excell, now a school principal in Shoshone, Idaho. Delbert Rentfro, the custodian refused entry into Room 4, is retired.

All of the children in fifth and sixth grades on May 16, 1986, have graduated from high school. Several of the students prominently mentioned in the book have gone on to college via scholarship. Many of the boys accepted calls from their church to serve as missionaries in widely scattered places, including Brazil, Micronesia-Guam, Spain and Australia.

Travis Walker went on to become high school student body president. Said Travis: "I personally feel that in being spared as we were, we now have a responsibility to make something special of our lives."

Appendix I
"ZERO EQUALS INFINITY"

The following statement is a copy of David Young's philosophy distributed to Cokeville students and teachers the afternoon of May 16, 1986. Similar copies were mailed to the press and to then-President Ronald Reagan. It is reproduced here exactly as written by Young himself. (His paper allowed only a 3/8" left margin and ran off the page on the right side. His infinity symbols were hand-drawn.)

Zero Equals Infinity

Seemingly, some thousands of years ago, several individuals combined, or perceived their combination and therein created Man.

This creation was, and is, a concept; a thought or idea, neither right or wrong (left) but a way among ways.

For the better part of the interim then, men played with Man making love, fire, food, mores, children, Gods, language, tools, wastes, etc: combinations of divers sorts, in almost as many directions (purposes). Now people come and people go, but always as people, no longer as individuals from which people had risen (or succumb). Almost as frequently as people come and go, additional, more distant concepts (from whatever reality is the individual/that precedes them); families, clans, tribes, villages, towns, cities, states, and civilizations make their brief passages and then leave the scene.

These various combinations of Man with their various concepts of themselves invented war in order that any singular combination might achieve dominance over other combinations. This came to pass as Man attempts to preempt those rights of the individual. The individual remembers reality only in learned (rather than the original and innate, therefore false) responses to right (his combinations values) and wrong (other combinations values differing from his own.)

History is the study of these combinations.

As a matter of record, therefore, some 2400+ years ago, Socrates, an individual, addressed himself to an evolving concept called knowledge. Knowledge is again a way to conceive, but conception is enlarged through rules less combination specific. Philosophy, remote as ever, is slowly displaced by science (mathematics, medicine, astronomy, etc.), a disciplines observing the singular rule that a fact becomes knowledge when it can be proved.

Proof is a concept, it suggests something that "is" on account of itself—it "is" proven. At best a probability, at worse nonsense, proof in any event is very distant from reality. Nevertheless it has been the predominant concept these 2000+ years and any combination that has competed with other combinations using it has eventually either adopted it or ceased to exist.

Be this as it may, knowledge and its attendant proofs

remain but a way among ways. Socrates, reputed to be the wisest man of his time, investigated the basis of knowledge in a manner still available (Plato wrote it down and it survives), still as viable, and still as conclusive as it was 2400+ years ago. Socrates concluded, just as we must, "As for me, all I know is that I know nothing."

Nothing? This knowledge of 'nothing' then is all we have for all the lessons of history, these 2400+ years, Christ, revolutions, insurance, relativity, moon and space probes, crusades and inquisitions, Shakespeare, Newton, medical science, hydrogen, fusion, metallurgy, Hitler, electricity, government and law, etc.?

The answer to this concern regarding the nothingness of knowledge is rather yes and no. The Knowledge of Nothing is all there is (to know), but 99.9% of us don't even know that. Mostly, as in all these several thousands of years, we believe (another concept!) we know that 2 plus 2 equals 4 or that a line perpendicular from the ground is up, or that Christ is good (bad or indifferent), or that our names or ages are such and such.

All these beliefs we accustom to call knowledge (and knowledge ordained to have been proven, yet!) we wont to impress on all combinations (peoples) for their (and our) collective salvation (moral integrity).

That our belief that the moon is something we can put men on, or that a certain creed offers a unique conclusion, or that $E=MC2$ is not one whit more true than a New Guinean tribes concepts and rationales that have preserved its stone age culture into our world, leave the majority of us feeling wronged. Therefore, rather than learn the reality and limitations of knowledge, we refute truth with some age old axiom (bullets conquer stone axes), note the bobbing heads of surrounding bigots (99.9% of eve-ryone) and retunr without doubt or question to selfish, self-centered, egotistical sub systems and social specific cultures from which we otherwise might free ourselves.

Were we to continue, however, the investigation of knowledge, we'd need to interna-lize Socrates': All I know is that I know nothing. 0 = [infinity symbol], Zero (or Nothing) Equals the Infinite. TRUTH!

How is this to be? Believing 2pplus 2 equals 4 hardly invalidates Knowing 0 = [infinity symbol]. The diabolical trick we've otherwise learned (internalized) is realativity; when in Rome do as the Romans, when doing math do as the mathematicians, when fighting a thermonuclear war, discard spears and arrows for the thermonuclear devises, etc.

While 2 plus 2 equals 4 (and there would have been no men put on the moon if it hadn't) it might just as well equal 22 or many ('primitive' tribes frequently respond thus to any mathematical concept above 3) or various other concepts that are easier to ignore than to realize, know, and internalize. But would we internalize these various concepts, we realize the relativeness of these various formulas, that knowledge is indeed relative, therefore untrue, therefore unknowledge, certainly nothing unless falsehood.

That 0 = [symbol for infinity] is TRUE, REALITY, and a

symbolic manner of rephrasing Socrates' conclusion regarding the limits of knowledge is another matter. Here we confront what we thought we pursued all these years, what we should have remembered from 2400 years ago. The imortal Greek told us, showed us, and taught us the limitations of knowledge and we killed him for it, not merely one individual once, but in all this nonsense we've engaged in since. Still, 2400 years, 24,000 years, or 240,000 eons, there is truth-relativity and TRUTH. Let's cease to be beasts and begin to be Gods!

As was suggested at the beginning of this writting, Man is an invention, he is lots of individuals. Rather or not individuals ultimately exist (and what we mean by asking that question) is matter for another writting, it will presently suffice to remember that we still singularly (individually) conceive and perceive in the ever-present. Aware of the relativity of the games we play in our various existances, we will allow our individual trajectories (precepts and concepts) their original and innate freedom to achieve their own accords (determine their own natures) without the hindrances of Man, families, clans, villages, towns, cities, states, or civilizations.

Responsible, as ever (we die our own death, remember?) for our own actions (no Man, family, clan, village, town, city, state, government, or religion condoning withholding the above noted original and innate freedoms) we will collectively evolve into the next step of wherever it is we're going (Nowhere in the REALITY of 0 = [symbol for infinity] but still a long was from achieving it.).

"We are all ONE and 'we' came apart to do 'this' for something 'to do' in Nothing and Infinity."

David G. Young
4/th Oct. 1978
Tucson, Arizona

LIST OF FOURTEEN FACTORS

The following is a list of fourteen factors, compiled by bomb expert Richard Haskell and his co-investigators, which mitigated the fatal effects of the deadman's bomb designed by David Young.

1. The connecting wires to the lower set of blasting caps had been cut through cleanly, preventing battery current from reaching the caps and detonating them. This reduced the amount of gunpowder sprayed into the room on detonation by 40%.

2. The two blasting caps which did not detonate were placed on a lower shelf than the three which did, thus preventing them from being triggered by the bomb's heat.

3. The soft ceiling tile absorbed much of the overhead heat.

4. The two small windows were open, which helped vent at least part of the bomb's initial concussive force.

5. The two hallway doors were also open, which had a further dampening effect.

6. The tables and chairs had been moved from the center of the room, which allowed the children to more quickly escape the initial impact of the fireball.

7. No one was sitting or standing directly against the walls, where the main combustive force of the blast traveled after spreading across the ceiling.

8. None of the children were standing or sitting in the 10' x 10' taped-off "magic square," surrounding the bomb, and were thus slightly distant from the effects of the initial explosion.

9. David Young selected, for some reason, a plastic jug that leaked; he then did not notice the leak when he filled the jug with gasoline. Further, he did not see or smell the leaking gas all afternoon, even when he was sitting or standing next to the jug. Most importantly, the leaking gas turned some of the explosive particles into paste, preventing their becoming air-borne or igniting when the bomb went off, further minimizing intended damage.

10. Doris's body apparently absorbed much of the explosion's fury, as she was standing between the bomb and the hostages.

11. The children had had a school-wide drill just the week before in the school cafeteria "on how to escape a fire quickly from a single room."

12. Princess gave an early warning to authorities, including critical details about the guns and the bomb her father had brought into the school. Civil Defense workers who had the necessary contact network to begin proper response to the emergency "just happened" to be on hand to coordinate it.

13. The hostages wisely chose to wait out the dilemma

rather than risk being shot trying to escape or rushing David Young. To have done the latter would have left them more exposed to the close-in, maximum explosive force of the bomb.

14. Despite the dense smoke, the teachers did just the right thing at the right time, at the windows and doors, to evacuate all the children from every part of the room before anyone had time to succumb to the pain, fire, or lack of oxygen.

The following list includes a number of related "coincidences," pointed out by various people, both hostages and authorities, that should have resulted in fatalities, but did not.

• After looking at the bombed-out room, Richard Haskell concluded over and over again that, even in the partial explosion which did occur, it was unexplainable that no one died in the concussion, flames or smoke which exploded in such a small area.

• Music teacher John Miller was shot with the smaller of the two weapons David Young was holding, not the more lethal one. The bullet penetrated near, but not into, Miller's heart; he was out of the hospital in two days.

• Billie Jo Hutchinson's injuries put her in grave danger for weeks, yet she finally recovered. Likewise, Tina Morfeld almost died from her internal injuries, but also recovered.

• Gina Taylor's badly burned right eye healed better than anyone could predict, overturning medical opinions that she would probably have life-long impairment from the injury.

- David Young had Eva Clark immediately in front of him and was pointing his guns at her. Yet even when she turned her back on him to shepherd her children out of the room, he did not fire on her.

- Jean Mitchell was standing next to Doris Young when the bomb went off but inexplicably escaped instantly catching on fire as Doris did.

Appendix III

LIST OF HOSTAGES

Afternoon Kindergarten
Sam Bennion
Paul Clark
Heather Cory
Linzie Jo Conner
Jodie Eggleston
Jamy Ferrin
Trini Jo Himmerich
Julia Jamison
Joshua Jones
John King
Jody Pope
Bret Taylor
Gina Taylor
Joshua Wiscombe

Grade 1A
Jolene Buckley
Fawna Eastman
Carl Grandy
Nathan Hartley
Hilary Larson
Joni Larson
Travis McKinnon
Jeremiah Moore
Emily Murdock

Collin Roberts
Shawn Stahl
Ryan Taylor
Katie Walker

Grade 1B
Shelley Burton
Burton Clark
Jennifer Cory
Billie Jo Hutchinson
Chad Hymas
Brenna McNamara
Kevin Nate
Shiloh Pope
Heather Prows
Jennie Sorensen
Meaghan Thompson
Jeromy Lamb
Jay Metcalfe

Second Grade
Clark Bedell
Nancy Bennion
Cameron Bird
Brandon Brooks

Jennie Buckley
David Burton
Melanie Chadwick
Michelle Coates
Wade Cornia
Tareesa Covert
Jodi Dayton
Carl John Eggleston
Jason Hartley
Austin Henderson
Jamie Himmerich
Nanette Holden
Chad Madsen
Kellie Miller
Tina Morfeld
Levi Murdock
Karee Thornock
Ryan Thornock
Willie Wathen
Byron Wiscombe

Third Grade

Andy Bagaso
Jamie Buckley
Matthew Buckley
Justin Chadwick
David Clark
Joelle Dana
Ranelle Dana
Hyrum Esterholdt
Jenny Ferrin
Cindy Hartley
Billy King

Heather Larson
Joe McNamara
Chad Mitchell
Kristi Moore
Scott Mower
Aaron Roberts
Joey Sweat
Michael Thompson
Karalyn Thornock
Rachel Walker

Fourth Grade

Rusty Birch
Jerry Dayton
Dustin Eastman
Ricky Himmerich
Lana Holden
Adam Hymas
Sandy Hymas
Jeana Jamison
Joe Mackey
Jaime Metcalfe
Monica Morfeld
Jamie Taylor
Jason Thornock
Kimberly Thornock
Stephanie Wiscombe

Fifth Grade

Amy Bagaso
Janaan Bennion
Elisabeth Clark
Shaneil Cornia

BranDee Hess
Jeromy Jamison
Amber Larson
Colton McDermott
Joanna Metcalfe
Brad Shane Nate
Lori Nate
Angie Nostaja
Adam Prows
Justin Sweat
Michael Taylor
Leigh Ann Thornock
Travis Walker

Sixth Grade
Kent Cassels
Christy Clark
Tammy Coates
Allyson Cornia
Drew Cornia
Celeste Excell
Brenda Hartley
Brandi Himmerich
Paul Lazcanotegui
Kimberly Madsen
Bobbie Jo Miller
Brian Nate
Greg Nate
Cameron Roberts
Heidi Roberts
Anna Stewart
Kyle Thornock
Kamron Wixom

Others
Pat Bennion, substitute teacher
Verlene Bennion, teacher's aide
Gayle Chadwick, media aide
Eva Clark, parent
Kathy Clark, preschooler
Tina Cook, secretary
Cynthia Cowden, teaching job
    applicant
Sandy Gonzales, UPS driver
Kris Kasper, student teacher

Teachers
Max Excell, Principal
Janel Dayton
Kim Kasper
John Miller
Jack Mitchell
Jean Mitchell
Rocky Moore
Gloria Mower
Carol Petersen
Kliss Sparks

*Cokeville Elementary Students
absent May 16, 1986*
Chris King, first grade
Wendy Bartschi, second grade
Vern Setser, third grade
Mandy Taylor third grade
Julie Anderson, fourth grade
LeaKae Roberts, fourth grade

Morning Kindergarten Students

Josh Anderson
Amanda Birch
Candice Bird
Zack Bird
Alex Dayton
Jessica Dayton
Chris Esterholdt
Mindi Hymas
Sandra Metcalfe
Julie McKinnon
Ben Pieper
Brittany Swenson
James Thompson
Krista Thornock
Phillip Stoker
Dain John
Jared Sweat
Regina Tso

Appendix IV

SOURCES OF INFORMATION

Personal Interviews and Statements:
Glen Birch family (home used by media), statement of
    May 18, 1986
Eva Clark (hostage/mother of hostages), interviewed
    May 18, 1986
Christina "Tina" Cook (hostage), interviewed May 24,
    June 10, 1986
Janel Dayton (hostage), interviewed May 22, 24, 1986
John Dayton (Cokeville mayor), interviewed May 24, 1986
School Principal Max Excell (hostage), interviewed May
    19, 1986
Ron Hartley (investigator), interviewed May 21, 30, 1986;
    March 12, 1994
Jack and Jean Mitchell (hostages), interviewed May 24,
    1986
Bernie Petersen (relation of Youngs), interviewed June
    10, 1986
Carol Petersen (hostage), interviewed May 24, 1986
Gwen Petersen (relative of hostage), interviewed May 22,
    30, 1986
Genera Robinson (home used by media), interviewed
    May 19, 1986
Kliss Sparks (hostage), interviewed May 24, 1986
Steve Taylor (father of hostage), statement of May 19,
    1986

Newspapers and Periodicals
  Arizona *Daily Star*
  Brigham Young University *Daily Universe*
  Color Country Spectrum
  Denver Post
  Salt Lake City *Deseret News*
  Kemmerer, Wyoming *Gazette*
  Las Vegas *Sun*
  Pueblo, Colorado *Chieftain*
  Provo *Daily Herald*
  Mormon Trail
  Newport, Virginia *Times-Herald*
  Rocky Mountain *News*
  Phoenix *Gazette*
  Salt Lake Tribune
  Star Valley Independent
  University of Utah *Chronicle*
  Utah Statesman
  Virginia *Pilot*
  Time Magazine

Hearings:

Under the jurisdiction of Lincoln County, Wyoming, County Attorney Richard Leonard conducted hearings at the county seat in Kemmerer. Hostages, witnesses and lawmen gave testimony. Leonard announced the investigation completed on February 5, 1987.

KAMRON WIXOM
"PRESS RELEASE"

"Press release" written by Kamron Wixom to help answer questions of concerned family and friends.

The BOMB
by Kam Wixom

COKEVILLE— (May 16, 1986) Our sixth grade class was on a bathroom break when a lady came up to us and said, "Go in the First Grade room, and we have a surprise for you." Our teacher, Mr. Mitchell, asked what kind of surprise. She said, "You'll find out."

The teachers told us the man in the room had bombs, and we thought it was an assembly, that he was an expert helping us get through a possible Libyan attack. He said he was the "most wanted man in the culture." That was about all he said. He talked privately with some of the teachers who went up to him, and we learned he and the woman were holding us hostage until they could get $2 million for each of us. There were about 150 students gathered in this one classroom.

The man had three pistols attached to his belt, and they

had two .22 rifles and an M1 leaning against the wall by the door. They had a metal shopping cart full of batteries, and an old milk jug filled with gasoline, and we could see metal wires for the trigger, some batteries, and copper coil inside. There were four or five explosives found later elsewhere in the school.

The sixth grade, and some of the younger kids around us agreed we should say a prayer. We were all sitting on the floor. We folded our arms and Allyson Cornia just started saying a prayer for us. She said she wanted everybody to be safe, that we would all survive. We felt we had done our part in asking the Lord to help us. Now it was up to us to cooperate and do all we could.

A lot of kids were crying softly. All of us were scared, but some didn't want to show it because we knew it wouldn't do us any good. I thought, "I just don't want to get in trouble and have the bomb go off." None of us ever thought about going out of the room even though we were near the door that had been propped open. We didn't want to do anything they didn't want us to do. We asked the teachers how long we would have to stay there. They said, "Maybe ten days, maybe just a couple more hours."

The teachers were trying to get our minds off it by letting us watch TV and read books, and play games like Legos™. Brenda Hartley and I built a tank out of Legos, complete with guns. I said to Brenda, "OK, men, we're going to cross the 'death lines' and blow'em up." The "death line" was the tape on the floor that Mr. Mitchell had placed around the bomb and the man sitting on the desk next to it. He had said, "OK kids, we are gong to play a game. This is the magic square, and if you pass it you'll be out." No one tried to get near the square. Brenda had laughed when I said what I did about our tank. Then we got up and went to the table near the door where some magnets were that we could play with.

We had all been in the room together now since about 1:30. It was now a little before 4. The man had called his wife to come and hold the trigger to the bomb, and he went into the bathroom which is connected to the classroom. He had been in there about two minutes. We were all beginning to feel a little more relaxed, then BOOM! I looked up and saw the ball of fire and a cloud of black smoke. The fire stayed low, but the smoke spread quickly through the room. There were pieces of paper in flames floating around the room, and falling in front of me. Everybody started yelling and running. I went out the door and ran north toward the main doors. I was the first one to go through those doors, and ran on toward Main Street saying softly to myself, "I'm alive!"

Our band teacher, Mr. Miller, had run out of the school through the south doors and was shot in the back by the man who had come out of the rest room when the bomb went off. Mr. Miller collapsed at the corner on Main Street near where I was standing.

There were ambulances, crowds of people searching for brothers and sisters with tears in their eyes. It was like I had come back into civilization after being out in the wilds alone. Kids were being hosed off to cool their burns. I went into

Steve Taylor's house to call home, but no one was there. I
went back out onto the street, looking for someone to leave a
message with that I was going to go down to city hall with
some of the other kids and get out of the crowd. That's when
I saw Dad with his arm raised, and Mom with her arms open.
I ran to them. I was sure glad to see them. Mom and I
hugged for a long time, then Dad caught up to us and we
had a three-way hug. I cried. It felt good to cry. I had been
too mad to cry before.

A PERSONAL CONNECTION

"This is the kind of entry no one—not in her wildest imaginations—figures she would make in her journal...Our son is one of the hostages." This is my wife's journal entry May 18, 1986.

Two days earlier our high school-aged daughter, Jenny, ran frantically into the house from the bus stop. Sobbing and calling almost hysterically to her mother, she gave the terrifying news.

"Did you hear? Don't you know what's happened?" Jenny cried. She and her best friend Carrie Anderson were confused and grief-stricken. Their faces displayed the stunned disbelief they felt. "Some people with bombs are holding the elementary school hostage!"

"My mind went blank," wrote my wife, Judene, in her journal. "I was annoyed with the girls for going too far with one of their pranks. This was, well, just too absurd? They're full of pranks, but their grief was all too real. I had to believe them. I was numb with disbelief.

"I sat down with them, trying to comfort them while at the same time trying to sort this out in my head. Nothing sorted.

"I felt so...alone, confused, frustrated. In desperation, I fell on my knees and pleaded for help that the children would somehow find the courage they needed to withstand this ordeal. I felt relief—I was afraid to feel assured," the journal entry concluded.

I hadn't seen my wife in five days. For the first time I had commuted home early for the weekend from Provo, Utah, where I was working as student newspaper advisor at Brigham Young University.

The only hint I had of anything wrong came as I approached Cokeville and headed toward my home about six miles north of town. A normally conservative neighbor sped past me going about eighty miles per hour. I thought I noted a worried look on his face but figured it was just a personal matter.

Instinctively, I checked my own speedometer and continued driving. It seemed like a peaceful afternoon. There was no particular reason to hurry.

Judene had just watched two ambulances and a police car speed past on the highway in front of the house. As I turned down our driveway, she was conversing with Cindy Dayton, who had been a substitute teacher at the high school that day. Her tear-streaked face showed her desperate desire to just "wake up from this whole thing."

Spotting me, my wife came running up the driveway. As she threw herself into my embrace with more intensity than ever before, I first thought this was the kind of greeting I had always wanted. But seeing her face filled with anguish kept me from enjoying it.

"Is everything all right?" I asked, looking into her eyes.

"No! The grade school kids are being held hostage by someone with a bomb…. They want millions of dollars. They have guns...." The scenario gushed out in a flood.

"What?" I found myself saying.

"Our son is in there...!"

When my wife told me that, I first envisioned an idle threat, a fake bomb. Passersby who had maybe swallowed too much Percodan.

My mind turned to the practical; we would need to take sleeping bags and several days' food to wait at the school yard entrance. If the extortionists took a child to make their getaway...well, it would complicate getting everyone out of this unharmed.

It would do no good to speculate. We had to obtain more details about this strange dilemma.

The two of us were joined by our second high school-age daughter, Cindy, and Joanne Metcalfe, a neighbor who had three children in the classroom. The two mothers shared a hug; it was the only way to express the feelings words couldn't. Her husband, Jack, had taken his high school civics class on a field trip. Knowing she needed support from someone in this grotesque circumstance, we invited her to come inside the house.

Joanne called the school. When Max Excell answered, Joanne quickly blurted out, "What's going on there?"

"It's true! There is a man here with a bomb. I can't tell you much more—I've got to go." Joanne had no idea at the time how much pressure Excell was under to make every moment count.

In our living room there was a heavy silence mixed with confusion as we attempted to not assume the worst. Then

Joanne's high school-aged son Aaron burst in. "The bomb went off! Boom! I just heard it on the radio!"

The two families headed toward town in separate vehicles. I thought of Kam's smile the week before as he showed me his tree hut, his proud look when he brought in a gallon of milk from the dairy barn on a subzero morning, the last picture he had drawn of a "supercar of the future." The future....

I also thought of the children now being held hostage, the ones I had taught in the honors English class at mid-year. These fifth and sixth graders put out their own newspaper "wondering what we can use for exciting news."

Several of the students had also enthusiastically created stories which might be published in magazines elsewhere. One was a detective story about children in a small town being kidnapped. What a wonderful imagination, I thought.

The teachers—I had worked with them daily. My wife and I saw them frequently in almost every community activity. What was happening to them?

Probably every vehicle hurrying to the school grounds held people with similar thoughts. Many talked openly and freely of their anxiety to find out more, and when they did, they spoke of their feelings of helplessness. Most said unashamed prayers on behalf of the hostages and their families.

As I parked my car at the curb just outside the school grounds, I saw Dr. Allen Lowe, Lincoln County School District Superintendent, step from his vehicle. His face was ashen. Few words could be found. A voice on the radio came through the silence—something about parents searching for their children.... Here, in front of me, I saw it happening.

Children stood dazed, with a look of incredulity at being alive. Quilts and blankets were hastily gathered from nearby homes. They were being wrapped compassionately around shivering youngsters sitting on lawns, many of whom were waiting for a turn at oxygen tanks. There were ambulances everywhere.

Several children with blackened faces and arms were coughing from the effects of smoke inhalation.

It struck us immediately that although this was an unbelievable event, all the chaos was somehow transforming into precise organization. Everyone was functioning in his own field of expertise, and parents and neighbors were filling in the gaps. Teenagers were handing out blankets and cups of water.

Even though the paramedics came from different counties, they were working as if coordinating a drill.

The frantic faces wore the same wide-eyed expression. The horror of the event had not yet been fully realized, nor would it be for some time yet.

We both jumped out of the car and ran toward the center of activity. Looking through the frenzied crowd, I saw Kamron. He had been calling us from the Taylor's home on Main Street. It must have been an extremely lonely feeling for him to get no answer. He knew his mother would be worrying. His face showed no signs of burns. Just the blankness of shock. Feelings and reality had not yet meshed together.

I raised my hand up and called to him. He said I loomed out of the crowd "like a telephone pole." His eyes could see nothing else but his parents. He came running.

He reached his mother first. There were no words. Just an ecstatic embrace.

Later, mother and son looked at a photograph of that memorable reunion. The picture, taken by a television photographer, captured the elation and relief of the moment. It was circulated on network broadcasts and picked up by a wire service. The look on their faces so effectively told the story of this drama taking place that it ran in several newspapers around the country.

One of the papers to print it was the *Arizona Daily Star* in Tucson. Our oldest daughter, Wendi, lived in Safford, 140 miles northeast of Tucson, with her husband, Don, and daughters, Rachel and Evie. It had been two years since she had seen Kamron. A neighbor boy brought the paper to her home. "Is this your mom and little brother?" he asked Wendi, knowing she was from Cokeville. Wendi grabbed the boy and the newspaper all in one big, excited swoop, and gave both of them a hug.

She recognized the jacket her mother was wearing. "It was your camp jacket," she explained later. "I looked at that picture and thought how the jacket would smell of campfire, and all the fun times we've had on our outings came flooding back.

"The photo came alive to me," she said, "and helped me feel a part of the circle. I needed to be in touch with the family during this crisis."

In her excitement, she impulsively called the *Star* to thank them for the picture.

It was later, in the middle of Evie's two-year-old birthday party that the newspaper called Wendi with some more questions. That night the newspaper ran the same photo again with the headline, "Photo eases worry for Safford woman."

"It was the first time I could visualize my family was fine!" she told the paper.

Wendi had originally learned of the disaster from her husband, who heard reports on the radio. He hurried home to be with her before she got the news elsewhere. She said she had a foreboding all afternoon something was wrong. It might have been precipitated by the minor surgery her husband had a few days before, added to his having to drive a long way alone.

"I cried for an hour. Then Don came home and told me what he had heard. We called the home in Cokeville but couldn't find anyone. I finally reached a family friend in Cokeville, Leon Pope. He told me his sister, Jody, was burned, but that he heard Kam was all right."

In the meantime, hearing reports on our car radio about "a bomb exploding in a school classroom in Cokeville, Wyoming," we worried about what other relatives and friends might think. It would be very easy to imagine the worst. Family members in other states soon to get the six o'clock news might think Kam and his friends were killed. Yet we had managed to get only one call through to my mother in Salt Lake City. We were able to spare her concern before she even learned of the crisis, but we could get no further access to an outside line.

Leon had reached us to report Wendi's call. There was still Judene's mother, somewhere in New York on vacation, and our other married daughter, Julie, in Virginia. Two other children, Peggy and Wade, were working for the summer as guides on the Colorado River, away from telephones for a week or more. They must be informed.

Getting through to them seemed impossible. Telephone lines, of course, were jammed by many people trying to reach acquaintances that afternoon. My nephew Mark Pierson reached us from Salt Lake City by continually pushing the telephone redial button "until he got something besides a busy signal." Then he was able to alleviate fears of his own family.

Before the next thirty-six hours had concluded, our telephone bill, like many others in the area, soared to nearly $200.

As we continued our efforts to reach family members and friends, the reality of the day's events weighed on us heavily.

Kamron, now huddled in a quilt in the living room, had just answered extensive questions for many reporters, including some from Salt Lake City's *Deseret News*. The latter interview by Ellen Fagg and photographer Gerald Silver was sensitive and thoughtful. The atmosphere was subdued yet poignant in the reporter's opening lines.

"In a trailer home about six and a half miles from Cokeville, Wyoming, Kamron Wixom sits on a couch, cross-legged, with a patchwork quilt draped around his shoulders,"

Ellen wrote. "He just finished talking long-distance to a reporter from New York—not an everyday experience for the twelve-year-old Cokeville Elementary sixth grader. But neither is the bombing of a school room a common experience in this sleepy town of 550."

"I felt kind of mad. Now I feel shaky," Kamron told the reporters.

"I think...there may be more mental harm than physical," I interjected to the reporters.

"Will you be scared to return to school next week?" reporters asked Kam.

"Not really," he said, "because I know they're both dead."

But by now, Kamron was beginning to feel the "shakiness" he had earlier mentioned. He grew more quiet.

The phone rang. Peggy was calling from Moab, Utah. "What's going on there?" she asked Kamron.

"Yeah," Kam responded. What was insanity and what was reality?

"I mean, what happened?" Peggy asked.

"It was a bomb."

"Are you OK?"

"Yeah." She could almost hear him shrugging his shoulders. "No big deal," she thought. "The news must be sensationalizing it."

She'd had a stressful day herself. A mix-up with rides earlier in the day had left her stranded 50 miles from civilization. After walking barefoot for six miles along a dirt road, she hitched a ride with an acquaintance who happened to drive by and finally arrived at her destination. Exhausted, she headed directly for her room.

"Hey," her co-workers called. "There's something on the news about Cokeville!"

"No one even knows where Cokeville is," she thought to herself. "How could they have something on national news?"

After talking to Kamron, she still wasn't sure what was happening. It seemed to her there was a gap between the news on television and her eyewitness brother. She put a call in to her older brother, Wade, who was visiting his girlfriend, Amy Shifflet, in Pueblo, Colorado. Peggy figured he had seen the broadcast and would want to know that Kam was safe.

"Bomb kills two, injures 75 in Cokeville, Wyoming elementary school explosion... Details later." That was what Wade had heard. The report was factual and true. Yet he was only one of hundreds of family and friends outside of Cokeville who wondered just who the two dead were or how extensive were the injuries. "And not just Kamron." Wade later explained. "That was my town. Who of all I knew were numbered among the dead?"

Cindy had a very different experience. As a high school senior, she had been in the prayer circle held that afternoon. She rode with us to town and saw Kamron herself. She knew who was injured and that it was the terrorists who were killed. The incident had a very real impact on her life.

"It became a turning point for me," she was to later say. "I had been troubled for years with things I thought were major. But in comparison to this, they suddenly seemed so small.

"With the help of the psychological counseling made available to us, I gained some coping techniques. I also learned a new perspective about myself and others and quit demanding so much. It gave me space to grow and improve. I also saw for myself how very much people need people, and I became a warmer, more trusting person."

Julie finally got through from Virginia. She had been receiving some intensive military training away from home and returned just in time to catch the news report. "I heard 'Wyoming' mentioned and hurried in to catch the details out of curiosity," she explained. "Then they said 'Cokeville' and 'school kids' and I went cold."

Julie, with extensive medical training in the Navy, heard reporters say something about the hostages having "black on their bodies like hot oil." She was horrified. "I knew the painful and destructive power of such a thing," she said.

Speculation was traumatic for many members of Cokeville families scattered across the United States who were listening and waiting for details. Julie was gratified to finally learn the full story, particularly about her little brother's welfare.

That left only Judene's mother to get in touch with. The hope was that our nephew had managed to reach her somewhere, somehow.

We learned later that she had been watching television at a home of friends in Poughkeepsie, New York. Someone called her attention to the Cokeville story, and she watched incredulously for more details.

Her reaction was just as we had feared. "I couldn't quite grasp the reality of it all," she later said. She tried unsuccessfully for two hours to reach us in Cokeville.

She finally called Salt Lake and learned from Mark that he had spoken to us. Though still reeling from the inconceivable story, she had her fears temporarily alleviated.

The morning newspapers showed a picture of a mother and child emotionally embracing. "That's my daughter...and my grandson!" she exclaimed. The feeling was indescribable as she tried to deal with a whirl of facts. An explosion—in a grade school? Why? Hostages—ransom—but they're SAFE!"

Still, until Judene and her mom were able to embrace each other a week later, it was not really over.... Similar emotional-psychological repercussions were occurring with each of the hostage families as the shock waves reverberated across the nation.

A Cokeville native, Barbara Perry, was driving through Donner Pass with her husband. "We had been listening to tapes for about two hours," she said. "I suggested we tune in to catch a little news and heard what had happened in my home town. The broadcast out of California said two people in Cokeville had been killed after teachers and children were taken hostage."

Her husband described her as "frantic." She immediately began figuring the odds of those two dead people possibly being her sister and her sister-in-law, both teachers at the elementary school. When they reached a phone, they tried but failed to get through to Cokeville. It was thirty-six hours before they were finally able to learn the whole story.

Barbara's mother experienced her own alarm right there in town. Lois Dayton was tending grandchildren while daughter-in-law Cindy substituted at the high school. Lois was unaware of any excitement just three blocks away at the school.

"I answered a hurried knock at the door. It was Carlene Nuss, from across the street. 'Take my baby!' she said, and thrust the youngster in my arms. I had no idea what was going on. Minutes later, Cindy came in for her children. She was crying and so shaken that she couldn't speak. There I was, wondering why I had Carlene's baby, seeing Cindy nearly hysterical, and knowing nothing. All I could do was wait until Cindy was calm enough to explain. The anxiety I experienced in all this was horrible!"

Every story added impact to what was unfolding before us. How far-reaching would it be?

It brought to mind something Doris Young had told the children. "Think of this as an adventure...something to tell your grandchildren about." It was not quite what Mrs. Young had in mind. But if adventure can be defined as "a hazardous risk or a remarkable experience," at least she was right about that part before she died.

This "adventure" was to touch many outside the immediate community. Columnist Kathy Jones of the *Eastern Arizona Courier* recognized the psychological trauma. Following a conversation with our daughter in Arizona, she wrote: "Wendi's greatest wish was for some way she could help. With a disaster like a flood or tornado there would be work to do in cleaning up, she said. It would help her better deal with the emotions about the incident." But in this situation, there seemed nothing Wendi could do, the column emphasized.

Wendi kept asking her younger brother on the telephone, like many family members living far away asked loved ones, "Are you sure you're OK?"

For Wendi, it would require a hug, real and physical with her hostage brother, before the tensions could be released.

Many families would deal with the trauma in different ways. Some would take the attitude they did when the temperature dipped to fifty below, or when kicked by a cow: "When the going gets tough, the tough get going." In the past, I had inclined toward the "just-grit-your-teeth" types. Over the years, my wife and I had seen many such joys and tragedies.

There was something different here, not only because it struck close to home, but because it was more than physical adversity. There was much emotional sorting out to do, not just for the hostages' personal feelings about themselves, but for others.

None of the hostage children had ever encountered so many new challenges within a single afternoon. This was not something they could turn off like TV.

This matter focused on a youngster's faith in himself and mankind. Trust and ability to love responsibly was, in essence, the future ladder to inner personal growth.

How would we respond to help our own son? Tougher or more lenient? With discipline? Just love?

It was mostly the latter. When our family moved to Provo to be closer to my work, we lived in a student housing area. In the warm summer nights, laughing and splashing in the pool next door could be heard until midnight. While it irritated my wife and me as we tried to get to sleep, it was sweet music to Kam's ears. People enjoying themselves meant no tension. He had much more difficulty getting to sleep after we moved from the student housing.

From it we gained a useful clue. He had experienced a lifetime of tension in one afternoon. Now he deserved something different. Harmony was the goal.

Several parents with children held hostage quickly saw that trying to force the memory away didn't solve their children's ills. Here was a matter to be more than reacted to—it had to be understood. For example, a child writing "CRAZY" and "INSANE" over a photograph of David Young's face might be a prosecuting attorney's nightmare, but it seemed excellent therapy to parents. When Kamron did just that, the entire family understood the full meaning behind the picture with the scribbled words on it.

The evening just before bedtime was not a good time for the former hostage son to be watching television. Terror, hostages, bombs, guns in Iran, Nicaragua, or elsewhere, represented former horror brought back to mind. Some teachers held hostage had to leave lights on at night. Parents felt sympathy was now in order for youngsters who had faced the same threat of death.

There was also the wonder of it. Judene reminded me that more people were accidentally killed leaving soccer games around the world than were seriously harmed by an exploding bomb and four guns. Maybe it was worth reflecting on with a degree of sympathy for these young hostages as often as they wanted it.

I also remembered something Janel Dayton told me: "During the actual crisis we had to be careful not to sympathize too much, or the children would take a clue from us that it was worse than they thought it was; but we gave a measure of sympathy, yes."

Concerning the many prayers said, I remember reading something Ralph Waldo Emerson had said about it: "Prayer is the contemplation of the facts of life from the highest possible point of view." Had the prayers of all these humble children on their knees toppled the kingdom of an arrogant philosopher on his tiptoes?

"Who could say it wasn't primarily the children's prayers which prevailed in the Cokeville crisis?" my wife asked. "If not that, what?"

These children were not fatalistic, I-can't-make-a-difference types at any time, it would appear. I thought of the space shuttle Challenger disaster where seven astronauts were killed. Some people might take the give-up attitude that things happen in a predestined manner, that it makes little difference what people do. Yet the Cokeville children thought they could make a difference by raising funds for the Challenger program—and in their minds they did.

The money raised was small but it showed the compassion the children had for the families of the Challenger victims. After all, one of them was a school teacher.

Whatever it was they had to do in the "Cokeville Incident," the kids persevered even if some did act like mere children as the afternoon wore on. They could take pride in being survivors.

As for lingering fears, it became increasingly clear it would do no good to attempt any rapid purge of them. One day Kam went to a movie, but this time there was little recollection about the film's story. A man sitting at the end of the aisle looked like David Young. Other children also "saw him" for months when they closed their eyes. Kam's concerns and the others would fade with time—and patient understanding.

Even after months went by, it required effort for Kam's long-distance sister. As a former school teacher, Wendi had thought school safe, like her home. She had the adult responsibility of coping bravely. Sometimes coping "bravely" could be a gigantic pain in the neck. She just wanted to be a little girl again, to forget logic, vent her feelings, and be rid of them. Tenderly, her father-in-law, Ernie Taylor, invited her to unload them on him. She did and she felt immediately better.

Peggy had the same experience, seven months later, as she placed the pages of this book onto a computer. She had managed to laugh about the day her raft flipped in a Colorado River rapid, leaving her gasping for breath in the stream's roaring white water. There she wondered for a time about her own survival.

Just a week later, May 16, she arrived home exhausted to learn she may have lost her little brother. "I could deal with the river and the rapids and the dangers. I knew what I was up against. Even something unexpected often had an explanation, a logical reason behind it.

"But the little kids, just going to school—they're all good kids just minding their own business. It didn't make sense. How could a person behave rationally and courageously toward something so completely irrational and cowardly?"

Many of her feelings could be multiplied by each of the hostage families at Cokeville.

Part of the therapy for everyone included learning more details of the incident—how the hostages won their trial by terror. With school and community psychologists offering service without cost to the parents or hostages, Judene took advantage of this opportunity to talk things over. It was the positive approach, meeting an obstacle and overcoming it.

Among the greatest rewards were the long hours spent with families absorbing spiritual events. This was not something to be taken lightly by anyone. It confirmed to witnesses that people still believe miracles happen in modern times. At the same time, my objective newspaper background was coming out. I teach journalism students to be skeptical, to question everything. "If your mother tells you she loves you, check it out," is the watchword. Yet here it was: one of the most amazing stories I'd ever repeated, exactly as I'd received it, objectively reported.

Our family had moved to Cokeville from the city to enjoy the experience of a small rural town. We had grown to love the people and the natural, human enrichment which became such an integral part of our lives. Best of all, Cokeville proved to be an excellent place to raise a family.

Having to move the summer following this town's crisis caused some emotional jarring. Ties were strong, and we have enjoyed the chance to return and visit on occasion. Several other families have moved, pulled away by economic necessity. The healing process continues within family units, wherever they have gone. Folks talk more willingly now of the trials they faced last spring. They continue to recall little details that shock and terror had partly clouded from their minds before.

The process of uncovering and recording facts of this story has been personally helpful in the long term as it forces the peeling away of emotional bandages. We have had to look at it objectively and in detail. It has given us something tangible to work with.

We discovered that the full impact of the crisis was not felt by many families, including ourselves, right at first. Some did not assess what was happening even as it was unfolding. I learned of one woman who had a grandchild in the hostage room, yet still made a trip out of town as planned.

"I just naively thought things would work out," she said. "When I realized later the entire story, I couldn't believe how nonchalant I had been."

I've thought since that her thinking was quite typical of Cokeville. People here are so optimistic and have such a we-can-do-it attitude that if two fell over a cliff, one would crack a joke to the other on the way down. Rub dirt where it hurts and don't let anyone see your frown.

One has to realize the presence of this self-reliant confidence in the town before comprehending the humorous comments made during the hostage ordeal— things like, "You're just going to die when you see that bathroom." It was a little room designed for little children. Of course, when they said that to David Young, they had no idea he was soon to shoot himself in that room.

The Cokeville incident was like a story which had been assigned to my own journalism students. First they received information about a girl losing her dog. Then they learned she was a blind girl. King was her seeing-eye dog. Suddenly, what was happening became much more meaningful when all the facts were in. In the Cokeville situation, the facts kept snowballing until those outside the hostage room began to understand what the people inside had really endured. Then, as it turned out, it was even worse than they thought.

Few inside the room wanted to talk of hating the perpetrators. They wanted to forget it. The best way to do that was not talk much about it—for a time. Then no one could keep it inside.

An intriguing facet from the researching on David Young was his search for the strong and the pinnacle of strength. To him it was to bolster himself and his environs with armor, guns, and explosives. In contrast, the hostages armed themselves with spiritual strength. The outcome proves which one was the more effective. It seems the Cokeville story is a classic one for finding such an answer—a modern David and Goliath event in history. True, for a time Young's definition seemed to prevail. Yet when those he used it on admitted their helplessness, they found strength sufficient enough to win.

With more information, perhaps we could find it easier to forgive and forget. Our son was not injured, but many